OXFORDSHIRE
CHRISTMAS

AN
OXFORDSHIRE
CHRISTMAS

DAVID GREEN

The
History
Press

First published 1992
This edition first published 2009

The History Press
The Mill, Brimscombe Port
Stroud, Gloucestershire, GL5 2QG
www.thehistorypress.co.uk

British Library Cataloguing in Publication Data.
A catalogue record for this book is available from the British Library.

ISBN 978 0 7524 5313 2

Typesetting and origination by The History Press
Printed in Great Britain

CONTENTS

from

LARK RISE
FLORA THOMPSON

Flora Thompson's classic trilogy comprising Lark Rise,
Over to Candleford *and* Candleford Green, *is a
charming and detailed evocation of a way of life in rural
Oxfordshire which has now long gone. It tells the story of
Flora's childhood and youth in the 1880s seen through the
eyes of her fictional counterpart Laura, when she lived in
the small hamlet of Juniper Hill – the Lark Rise of the
story. In this first extract she describes the simple pleasures
of a typical Lark Rise Christmas which, for most villagers, just about succeeded in distinguishing the festival from
any other day of the year.*

Christmas Day passed very quietly. The men had a
holiday from work, and the children from school, and
the churchgoers attended special Christmas services.
Mothers who had young children would buy them
an orange each and a handful of nuts; but, except at
the end house and the inn, there was no hanging
up of stockings, and those who had no kind elder
sister or aunt in service to send them parcels, got no
Christmas presents.

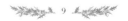

Still, they did manage to make a little festival of it. Every year the farmer killed an ox for the purpose, and gave each of his men a joint of beef, which duly appeared on the Christmas dinner table together with plum pudding – not Christmas pudding, but suet duff with a good sprinkling of raisins.

Ivy and other evergreens (it was not a holly country) were hung from the ceiling and over the pictures; a bottle of homemade wine was uncorked, a good fire was made up, and, with doors and windows closed against the keen, wintry weather, they all settled down by their own firesides for a kind of super-Sunday. There was little visiting of neighbours and there were no family reunions, for the girls in service could not be spared at that season, and the few boys who had gone out in the world were mostly serving abroad in the army.

There were still bands of mummers in some of the larger villages, and village choirs went carol-singing about the countryside; but none of these came to the hamlet, for they knew the collection to be expected there would not make it worth their while. A few families, sitting by their own firesides, would sing carols and songs; that, and more and better food and a better fire than usual, made up their Christmas cheer.

But there was one occasion when the festive season at Lark Rise had its lighter side too, although it was short lived. Even this, as Flora Thompson relates, was influenced by the nagging poverty which afflicted

*so many rural communities in the Oxfordshire of
Victorian England. She describes it as the episode of
the barrels of beer.*

At that time in that part of the country, brewers' travellers, known locally as 'outriders', called for orders at farmhouses and superior cottages, as well as at inns. No experienced outrider visited farm labourers' cottages; but the time came when a beginner, full of youthful enthusiasm and burning to fill up his order book, had the brilliant idea of canvassing the hamlet for orders.

Wouldn't it be splendid, he asked the women, to have their own nine-gallon cask of good ale in for Christmas, and only have to go into the pantry and turn the tap to get a glass for their husbands and friends. The ale cost far less by the barrel than when bought at the inn. It would be an economy in the long run, and how well it would look to bring out a jug of foaming ale from their own barrel for their friends. As to payment, they sent in their bills quarterly, so there would be plenty of time to save up.

The women agreed that it would, indeed, be splendid to have their own barrel, and even the men, when told of the project at night, were impressed by the difference in price when buying by the nine-gallon cask. Some of them worked it out on paper and were satisfied that, considering that they would be spending a few shillings extra at Christmas in any case, and that the missus had been looking rather peaked lately, and a glass of good beer cost less than doctor's physic, and that maybe a daughter in service would be sending a postal order, they might venture to order the cask.

Others did not trouble to work it out; but, enchanted with the idea, gave the order lightheartedly. After all, as the outrider said, Christmas came but once a year, and this year they would have a jolly one. Of course there were killjoys, like Laura's father, who said sardonically: 'They'll laugh the other side of their faces when it comes to paying for it.'

The barrels came and were tapped and the beer was handed round. The barrels were empty and the brewer's carter in his leather apron heaved them into the van behind his steaming, stamping horses; but none of the mustard or cocoa tins hidden away in secret places, contained more than a few coppers towards paying the bill.

When the day of reckoning came, only three of the purchasers had the money ready. But time was allowed. Next month would do; but mind! It must be forthcoming then. Most women tried hard to get that money together; but, of course, they could not.

The traveller called again and again, each time growing more threatening, and, after some months, the brewer took the matter to the county court, where the judge, after hearing the circumstances of sale and the income of the purchasers, ordered them all to pay twopence weekly off the debt. So ended the great excitement of having one's own barrel of beer on tap.

from

THE CHRISTMAS BOOK
GYLES BRANDRETH

*Gyles Brandreth is a former Oxford scholar, President
of the Oxford Union, Artistic Director of the Oxford
Theatre Festival, founder of the British Pantomime
Association, creator of the National Scrabble
Championships, one-time European Monopoly
Champion, and holder of the world record for the longest-
ever after-dinner speech. It lasted twelve and a half hours!
He is also a well-known broadcaster on radio and television, a contributor to many newspapers and magazines,
and was elected as a Member of Parliament in 1992.
Among his numerous books is* The Christmas Book,
*published in 1984, which tells us just about everything
we are ever likely to want to know about Christmas, and
how to enjoy it. In the following extract, Gyles Brandreth
puts the origins of our annual celebrations into their
historical perspective.*

Christmas is special. Christmas is magic. It is a time
of warmth and peace. A season when we can revel
unashamedly in nostalgia and tradition. The cynics
amongst us have described Christmas as a period of
preparations, invitations, anticipations, relations, frus-
trations, prostration and recuperation! But to most of

us it is, above all else, a time of celebration. It always has been, and let's hope it always will be.

In the Christian world Christmas is celebrated in remembrance of the birth of Christ. It is literally the 'Mass of Christ'. Yet, strangely, the rituals associated with this religious festival are of pagan origin and were celebrated long before Christ was born.

Since time immemorial it has been in Man's nature to worship *something*, and because all life seems so dependent on that burning ball of fire in the sky, so vital to the success of harvests, early man went down on his knees and prayed to the sun. In the winter, the strength of the sun being less, it became necessary to slaughter animals for food, and these became the first religious sacrifices. In December, the annual rebirth of the sun turned into an important festival, and many traditions and rituals became established. In Rome on 25 December the *Dies Natalis Invicti Solis* was celebrated – the Birthday of the Unconquered Sun – sacred to Mithras, the god of light, and to Attis, the Phrygian sun god.

The festival was known as the Saturnalia and was a period of celebrations from 17 December right through to the New Year (Kalends) when the Latins rejoiced that the days were getting longer and the power of the sun stronger. It was a time of real merrymaking, when bonfires were lit, homes were decorated with special greenery, people gave each other presents, and there were lots of fun and games. Not blowing up balloons and playing video games,

Bringing in the yule log, an ancient Norse tradition which, for many, is still echoed when logs are burned in the modern Christmas hearth

but an early form of charades in which slaves dressed up as their masters, and lords pretended to be servants, and it is said that people danced through the streets wearing very little but blackened faces and a smile!

These pre-Christian celebrations didn't just take place in ancient Rome, for at the same time in Europe the winter solstice, when the sun is farthest from the equator and at a point when it appears to be returning, became known as the Festival of Yule. In Britain, France (Gaul), Germany, Denmark, Sweden, and especially Norway, the Yule or 'Juul' celebrations became the highlight of the year. Yule logs and candles were lit to the gods Odin and Thor, houses were decorated with evergreens, Yule food and drink were prepared, and mistletoe was ceremoniously cut. Although over two thousand years old, the Yule traditions are still continued today.

In Britain the Druids celebrated the Festival of Nolagh, and it is thought by some that Stonehenge was built as a temple to the sun, constructed in such a way that it cast shadows wherever the sun happened to be. In fact, practically every country in the world, from China to India, from South America to the Middle East, held celebrations at this time of year. In Greece it was the birthday of Hercules, Ceres and Bacchus (an excuse to indulge in the grape); the Egyptians claimed it as the feast day of Horus; it was not until the fourth century that Pope Julius I decided that 25 December should be celebrated as the birthday of Jesus Christ, and Christmas as we know it began.

We now celebrate Christmas every year, but with a little bit of pagan tradition, a Norse Yule log, Druid candles, a drop of wine from Saturnalia, and a feast from the winter solstice. The evergreens and mistletoe still decorate our homes, and each year we continue to give presents to those we love. That's the magic of Christmas.

THE BAMPTON MUMMERS
John Norton

*The ancient custom of performing mummers' plays at
Christmastime still survives in many parts of the country,
but in few places with as much enthusiasm as in the
Oxfordshire village of Bampton. In 1991 writer and journalist John Norton carried out a study of this colourful
rural tradition, from which the following account is taken.*

The mummers' tradition in Bampton has deep roots,
and records show that the customary Christmas
play was regularly performed for many years without a break right up to the beginning of the Second
World War.

The war, of course, put a stop to such merriment,
but in 1946 efforts were made to revive the old
custom. The words of the traditional play had always
been memorised by those taking part, and handed
down from year to year, but after the break caused by
the war, it was necessary to ensure that the authentic
version would still be used.

By relying on the memories of those who had previ-
ously taken part, the story was pieced together again, and
in the 1960s it was faithfully written down, the first time
it had ever been committed to paper. As a result, the old
tradition was able to continue, and the play still survives
in its original form to this day.

In the very early postwar years, the revived play was performed by local children instead of adults, and one of these was Don Rouse, who became involved in 1948 at the age of eleven, and who has been associated with the mummers ever since.

'Up to the 1960s,' he recalled, 'we performed on two days instead of just the one which we do now. On Christmas Eve we went round the big houses, and on Boxing Day it was the turn of the pubs. Then, with family commitments and other pressures, we had to cut down the number of performances, and confined them to Christmas Eve alone. In the early days it was traditional for people to stay at home and decorate their houses on Christmas Eve, but by the 1960s things had changed, and everyone was in the pubs on Christmas Eve – a much more rewarding day for us to go round! Originally, any money we were given went into our own pockets, but nowadays we collect for a local Bampton charity which helps the elderly and gives them a party each Christmas.'

The mummers' Christmas Eve timetable is a tight one, as they have no less that eight local pubs to visit as well as several houses. The play lasts about a quarter of an hour or so, and the first performance starts at about 5 o'clock. The aim has to be to reach the final pub before closing time – not an easy task when the mummers receive more than a little seasonal hospitality at each of the eighteen or so places where they perform.

The play itself has parts for ten characters – Father Christmas, Soldier Bold, Turkish Knight, Royal

The Bampton Mummers perform their traditional Christmas play in one of the village houses

Apprussia King, St George, Doctor Good, Little John, Tom the Tinker, Robin Hood and Jack Finney. As there are only six players, four of them have to double up, and this contributes to the general mirth among the audiences, even though there can be few people in Bampton who do not know the play almost as well as the mummers themselves.

The story alludes to the triumph of good over evil, and involves two fights, two deaths, and two resurrections performed by the versatile Doctor Good and Jack Finney, as well as plenty of comedy. The opening lines, spoken by Father Christmas, set both the scene and the mood:

In comes I old Father Christmas, welcome or welcome not.

I hope old Father Christmas will never be forgot.

There is a time for work, there is a time for play,

A time to be melancholy and for to be gay.

A time to be thrifty, a time to be free.

And sure enough this Christmas time we all shall jovial be.

For this is the time when Christ did come, that we might happy be.

The play inevitably provides a great deal of seasonal fun for participants and audiences alike, but despite all the hilarity, the mummers themselves do take the performances seriously. They realise they are perpetuating an ancient and colourful rural custom, without which Bampton – and other villages where the mumming tradition survives – would undoubtedly be the poorer at Christmastime.

The popularity of the mummers shows no signs of abating. In fact, as Don Rouse pointed out, 'some of the places where we perform are so crowded that we often don't have enough room to fall down and die!'

But this hardly seems to matter. There is a delightfully informal atmosphere about the proceedings, and the spirit of the festive season overrides everything. By the time the performers gather for the final song, the audience is left in no doubt that a merry Christmas is the order of the day:

Now for the music and now for the fun,
The feast is ready and Christmas is come,
So welcome us now, and give us a cheer,
For ol' Father Christmas comes once in a year.

THE CHRISTMAS TREE
C. Day Lewis

Cecil Day Lewis, regarded as one of the 'Thirties Group'
of poets together with W.H. Auden and Stephen Spender,
was Professor of Poetry at Oxford from 1951 to 1956. His
descriptive verse The Christmas Tree *is a delightful*
seasonal offering.

Put out the lights now!
Look at the Tree, the rough tree dazzled
In oriole plumes of flame,
Tinselled with twinkling frost fire, tasselled
With stars and moons – the same
That yesterday hid in the spinney and had no fame
Till we put out the lights now.

Hard are the nights now:
The fields at moonrise turn to agate,
Shadows are cold as jet;
In dyke and furrow, in copse and faggot
The frost's tooth is set;

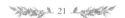

And stars are the sparks whirled out by the north wind's
    fret
On the flinty nights now.

So feast your eyes now
On mimic star and moon-cold bauble:
Worlds may wither unseen
But the Christmas Tree is a tree of fable,
A phoenix in evergreen,
And the world cannot change or chill what its mysteries
    mean
To your hearts and eyes now.

The vision dies now
Candle by candle; the tree that embraced it
Returns to its own kind,
To be earthed again, and weather as best it
May the frost and the wind.
Children, it too had its hour – you will not mind
If it lives or dies now.

from

THE ENGLISHMAN'S CHRISTMAS
J. A. R. PIMLOTT

*In 1960, the social historian John Pimlott, a former
open scholar at Worcester College, Oxford, wrote* The
Englishman's Christmas *as part of a trilogy on the history of British leisure. It was published a few years later
after the text was revised and updated by Dr Ben Pimlott.
The Victorian attitude towards Christmas inevitably
received a good deal of attention from the author, and in
these first extracts from the work he looks at the revival of
the singing of Christmas carols. Although today an inseparable part of our Christmas celebrations, the custom was in
danger of dying out in the last century had it not been for
the efforts of such men as the Reverend Henry Ramsden
Bramley, a Fellow at Magdalen College, Oxford, and
John Stainer, organist at the same college.*

Even if Christmas had been less important as a social
institution, the religious revival would presumably
have restored its place in the lives of churchgoing
people. There can, however, be no doubt that the
churches were all the fuller because of the immense
popularity of the secular Christmas.

Attendance at church became part of the
Christmas Day ritual of the middle classes, and as the

'In his master's steps he trod…' An original engraving by F.A. Fraser illustrating 'Good King Wenceslas' in the Victorian collection of carols compiled by Bramley and Stainer

ideas of the Oxford reformers spread, more communion services were held and more people took the sacrament. If the working classes in the towns were poorly represented, the reason was either that they were Nonconformists, or that they were permanently alienated from organised religion. But those who had been to church schools or Sunday schools had at least some instruction in the Gospel story and the meaning of the Nativity.

Taking everything together, the result was a wider and deeper awareness of the religious significance of Christmas, probably than ever before.

The Christmas bells, always a delightful feature of the English Christmas, rang out with a fuller meaning. For Tennyson they were 'the merry, merry bells of Yule', bringing sorrow touched with joy. 'Wake me tonight, my mother dear', wrote John Keble,

> That I may hear
> The Christmas bells, so soft and clear.

It was in the borderland between the religious and the secular festival that the Christmas carol was rediscovered. It is hard to realise how nearly the singing of carols had died out. The very title had a charm to the

Another of F.A. Fraser's engravings in the Bramley and Stainer carol collection. This one illustrates the carol 'Come Ye Lofty'

'God Rest Ye, Merry Gentlemen.' The Victorian engraver T. Dalziel produced this illustration for one of the Bramley and Stainer carols

'old-fashioned' ears of Mary Russell Mitford in 1840, and doubtless the same was true of Charles Dickens...

In 1868 William Henry Husk described carol singing as a departing custom and said that many spoke in the singular of '*the* Christmas carol' as though there were only one – 'God Rest Ye Merry, Gentlemen'.

It was because the carol was so obviously dying out that special importance attaches to the rescue operations which were begun by Bishop Percy with his *Reliques of Ancient English Poetry* in 1765 and continued in the early nineteenth century by Davies Gilbert, William Sandys and other antiquarians.

Thomas Wright, E.F. Rimbault and William Henry Husk were among those who kept up the work, and it has been followed up by later scholars and as part of the systematic collection of folk songs under the inspiration of Cecil Sharp.

The earliest attempts to resuscitate the custom were, however, unsuccessful. Small books of carols for church use which were published by Neale and Helmore in the fifties, and by Edmund Sedding in the sixties, made little impression. Husk, in 1868, referred to the occasional attempts of some of the clergy – 'anxious for the conservation of old customs' – to revive a taste for Christmas carols among their parishioners, and said that they had been too spasmodic to produce any successful result. They also seemed to have forgotten that 'no custom can be either established, sustained or revived by the mere desire of persons in authority. Unless the spontaneous wish of the people shall concur to give it vitality, it will soon droop and die'.

Once, however, the revival got under way it made rapid progress. The turning point came with the publication in 1871 of *Christmas Carols Old and New* by two young men, the Reverend H.R. Bramley, Fellow of Magdalen College, Oxford, and John Stainer, organist of the same college. It consisted of forty-two carols, some traditional and the majority by contemporaries. A later edition in 1878 contained seventy.

The music was designed for general use, and the value of the collection was mainly that it provided the

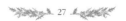

clergy with easily sung tunes with which they could supplement the ordinary Christmas hymns. As both Evangelicals and Anglo-Catholics were anxious to develop the singing of hymns and to take advantage of the popularity of congregational singing, religious controversy for once did not act as a brake upon innovation.

By 1885 it was possible for A.H. Bullen in his collection of carols, *A Christmas Garland*, to pronounce the cautious judgement that 'for some time past it has been a growing practice to sing carols in church instead of in the open air'. By the beginning of the new century, carol singing was widely popular among both Anglicans and Nonconformists.

from

WINTER IN THRUSH GREEN
Miss Read

'Miss Read' is the nom de plume of Dora Saint, a writer whose many books on country themes have earned her wide popularity. Among her best-loved works are the Thrush Green novels, relating stories about the life and times of a fictional village based on a real-life Oxfordshire community near Witney. Winter in Thrush Green, like its companions, paints an evocative picture of the

days when country living proceeded at a gentler pace than today, and there was more time to savour the delights and expectations of the Christmas season. In this first extract, Christmas is still two weeks away and the shops in the neighbouring town are in festive mood.

The little town of Lulling was beginning to deck itself in its Christmas finery. In the market square a tall Christmas tree towered, its dark branches threaded with electric lights. At night it twinkled with red, blue, yellow and orange pinpoints of colour, and gladdened the hearts of all the children.

The shop windows sported snow scenes, Christmas bells, paper chains and reindeer. The window of the local electricity showroom had a life-size tableau of a family at Christmas dinner, which was much admired. Wax figures, with somewhat yellow and jaundiced complexions, sat smiling glassily at a varnished papier mâché turkey, their forks upraised in happy anticipation. Upon their straw-like hair were perched paper hats of puce and lime green, and paper napkins, ablaze with holly sprigs, were tucked into their collars. The fact that they were flanked closely by a washing machine, a spin dryer and a refrigerator did not appear to disturb them, nor did the clutter of hair dryers, torches, heaters, bedwarmers and toasters, beneath the dining room table, labelled 'Acceptable Xmas Gifts'.

The rival firms of Beecher and Thatcher which faced each other across Lulling's High Street, had used

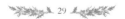

countless yards of cotton wool for their snowy scenes. Some held that Beecher's 'Palace of the Ice Queen' outdid Thatcher's tableau from Dickens's *Christmas Carol*, but the more critical and carping among Lulling's inhabitants deemed the Ice Queen's diaphanous garments indecent and 'anyway not Christmassy'.

Both firms had elected to have Father Christmas installed complete with a gigantic pile of parcels wrapped in pink or blue tissue paper for their young customers. A great deal of explanation went on about this strange dual personality of Father Christmas, and exasperated mothers told each other privately just what they thought of Beecher and Thatcher for being so pig-headed. The psychological impact upon their young did not appear to have dire consequences. Country children are fairly equable, and the pleasure of having two presents far outweighed the shock of meeting Father Christmas twice on the same day – once in the newly-garnished broom cupboard under Thatcher's main staircase, and next in the upstairs corset-fitting room, suitably draped with red curtaining material, at Beecher's establishment.

With only a fortnight to go before Christmas Day, Lulling people were beginning to bestir themselves about their shopping. London might start preparing for the festival at the end of October; Lulling refused to be hustled. October and November had jobs of their own in plenty. December, and the latter part at that, was the proper time to think of Christmas, and the idea of buying cards and presents before then was just plain silly.

'Who wants to think of Christmas when there's the autumn digging to do?' said one practically.

'Takes all the gilt off the gingerbread to have Christmas thrown down your throat before December,' agreed another.

But now all the good folk were ready for it, and the shops did a brisk trade. Baskets bulged, and harassed matrons struggled along the main street bearing awkward objects like tricycles and pairs of stilts, flimsily wrapped in flapping paper. Children kept up a shrill piping for the tawdry knick-knacks which caught their eye, and fathers gazed speculatively at train sets and wondered if their two-year-old sons and daughters would be a good excuse to buy one…

Christmas Eve arrives, and there is an air of excitement in the Thrush Green home of the Young family … then at last, night settles over the winter countryside and there's time to reflect on the meaning and promise of the day ahead.

Dusk fell at tea-time on Christmas Eve at Thrush Green. There was an air of expectancy everywhere. The windows of St Andrew's church glowed with muted reds and blues against the black bulk of the ancient stones, for inside devoted ladies were putting last-minute touches to the altar flowers and the holly wreath around the font.

Paul Young and his friend Christopher lay on their stomachs before the crackling log fire in the Youngs' drawing-room. They were engaged in fitting together a jigsaw puzzle, a task which Paul's mother had vainly hoped might prove a sedative in the midst of mounting excitement. They were alone in the room and their conversation ran along the boastful lines usual to little boys of their age.

'I never did believe in Father Christmas,' asserted Christopher, grabbing a fistful of jigsaw pieces which Paul had zealously collected.

'Here!' protested Paul, outraged. 'They're all my straight-edged bits!'

'Who's doing this?' demanded Christopher belligerently. 'I'm a visitor, aren't I? You should give me first pick.'

There was a slight tussle. Christopher twisted Paul's arm in a businesslike way until he broke free. Panting, Paul returned to the subject of Father Christmas.

'I bet you did believe in him! I just bet you did! I bet you *went on* believing in Father Christmas until I told you. So there! Why, I knew when I was four!'

'So what? I bet you still hang up your stocking!' bellowed Christopher triumphantly. Paul's crimson face told him that he had scored a hit.

'So do you,' retorted the younger boy, not attempting to deny the charge. They fell again into a delicious bear-hug, rolling and scuffling upon the hearth-rug, and finally wrecking the beginnings of the jigsaw puzzle which had been so painstakingly fitted together.

The sound of carol singing made them both sit up. Dishevelled, breathless, tingling with exercise and the

'The carol singers formed a tidy crescent round the doorstep'

anticipation of Christmas joys, they rushed into the hall.

The carol singers were a respectable crowd of adult inhabitants of Thrush Green, all known to the boys. So far this year the only carol singers had been one or two small children, piping like winter robins at the doors of the larger houses on Thrush Green for a few brief minutes, and then dissolving into giggles while the boldest of them hammered on the knocker.

The boys watched entranced as the carol singers formed a tidy crescent round the doorstep. Some held torches, and a tall boy supported a hurricane lamp at the end of a stout hazel pole. It swung gently as he moved and was far more decorative in the winter

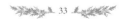

darkness, as it glowed with a soft amber light, than the more efficient torches of his neighbours.

Joan Young opened the front door hospitably, the better to hear the singing, and the choir master tapped his tuning fork against the edge of the door, hummed the note resonantly to his attentive choir, and off they went robustly into the first few bars of 'It Came Upon the Midnight Clear'.

Their breath rolled from their tuneful mouths in great silver clouds, wreathing about their heads and the sheets of music clenched in their gloved hands. In the distance the bells of Lulling church could be faintly heard, as the singers paused for breath.

The smell of damp earth floated into the hall, and a dead leaf scurried about the doorstep adding its whispers to the joyful full-throated chorus above it. The bare winter trees in the garden lifted their arms to the stars above, straining, it seemed to young Paul, to reach as high as St Andrew's steeple.

The boys gazed enraptured, differences forgotten, strangely moved by this manifestation of praise. It seemed to be shared by everything that had life…

Darkness thickened over Lulling and Thrush Green. The Christmas tree twinkled and blazed in the market square, dwarfing the stars above to insignificance.

Excited children for once went willingly to bed, stockings clutched in their rapacious hands, and heads whirling with delirious thoughts of joys to come. Exhausted shop assistants sat at home soaking their aching feet in warm water. The patients in Lulling

Cottage Hospital thought of the long gruelling day ahead, complete with boisterous surgeons carving turkeys, paper hats, hearty nurses singing carols, and all the other overwhelming paraphernalia of Christmas in the wards, and they shuddered or smiled according to temperament.

Housewives, flopping wearily in armchairs, congratulated themselves upon remembering the decorations for the trifle, the cherry sticks for the drinks, and other last-minute details, until they were brought up short by the horrid thought that in the pressure of so much unaccustomed shopping, they had completely forgotten salt and tea, and now it was too late anyway.

But away from the lights and worries of the town, the quiet hills lay beneath a velvety sky. No wind rustled the trees and no bird disturbed the night's tranquillity. Sheep still roamed the slopes as they had that memorable night so long ago in Palestine, and low on the horizon a great star, bright as a jewel, still held out an eternal promise to mankind.

HENLEY'S VICTORY CHRISTMAS
Ian Fox

*Christmas in 1918 was a very special one throughout
Britain, as it was the first to be celebrated in peacetime
after the horrors of the First World War which had ended
a few weeks earlier. At Henley-on-Thames the national
sense of relief was given a local slant by the* Henley
Standard *newspaper which, as Ian Fox discovered when
he delved into the archives, published this timely editorial
comment at the end of the festive season that year.*

There never was a Christmas like the one which
has just passed. Everything seemed so strange and
yet, withal, so real. For four long years the great war
cloud has hung over us and very few had any desire
to keep the old-fashioned time of peace and goodwill.
It would have been unpatriotic and unreal to have
indulged in festivity whilst our brave lads were on
the battlefield shedding their blood in order that we
might still maintain our freedom.

But the cloud has lifted and some of the former
gaiety associated with Christmas has returned,
although it will be a long while ere the yule log and
the mistletoe bough will form part of our festivities,
and the carollers will render their sweet melodies for
our delectation to the same extent as prevailed in
former years. True, the children have been doing their

Unfortunately, Henley's victory Christmas of 1918 was not blessed with such a rare experience as skating on the frozen Thames. This photograph was taken a few years earlier

little best in pleasurable anticipation of the coppers which generally rewarded their modest efforts. But what reminded one most of the returning to happier days was the playing of hymn tunes on the church bells last Sunday evening – a custom which prevailed on every Sunday in Advent in pre-war days.

Then, too, with increased stocks, the tradesmen have made a brave show of seasonable gifts and commodities, and, judging from the crowds which thronged the shops during the few days preceding Christmas Day, they must have had a splendid season.

In getting about the streets one would almost have imagined oneself in a garrison town, there being so much khaki and blue in evidence. This later fact was the cause of gratification not only to the relatives of the wearers, but to the townspeople generally, for in those lads they recognised brave fellows returned from the horrors of war, some of them men who had endured the barbarity of the Hun for many long weary months. Their welcome, although not adorned with civic state – that will, no doubt, come later on – was none the less hearty, it being quite the thing to hear in the streets the greeting heartily shouted, 'Cheer ho! How are you? Glad to see you home again.'

That word 'home' has a magic meaning at this season of the year, and the long holiday which most people are able to enjoy this year has been made the occasion in most homes of completing the family circle, although in many a cottage and mansion there are vacant chairs which, alas, will never be filled again, and whilst we are rejoicing in this our Victory Christmas, let us not forget those saddened homes and offer the occupants our sincerest condolences.

On Christmas Eve the fine bells of Henley parish church pealed forth merrily during the evening, and then at midnight their sonorous tones announced that once more the festival of 'Peace and Goodwill towards Men' had begun.

A lighter and more amusing seasonal comment –
although not, presumably, to the retired naval officer who
wrote it – appeared in the form of a letter to the same
Henley newspaper a few years later. It would seem to
have something of a timeless quality about it.

Christmas Carollers

Sir, – Cannot something be done to stop the nuisance caused by the boys and girls who nightly go round singing at this time of the year? They commence their operations weeks before Christmas (even before December is with us), and their singing is usually accompanied by an incessant hammering at the front door.

A few nights ago I passed three separate parties each making a different noise at houses almost next door to one another. The noises themselves are bad enough, but it really is intolerable when, as happened at my house tonight, one's disinclination to give what would only be an encouragement to them to come, or send others, again another night, was followed by a stone crashing through a window of the room in which my children were playing.

It surely should be possible to put some limits to these proceedings.

Yours faithfully,
M. T. DANIEL, Captain R.N. (retired).

St Michael's,
Henley-on-Thames.

17th December, 1924.

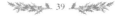

WINTER
Robert Southey

*The writer, historian and poet Robert Southey
(1774–1843) is one of the many great names of English
literature to have been associated with Oxford. He was at
Balliol College in 1793, and twenty years later, while still
in his thirties, he was created Poet Laureate. Among the
considerable volume of work he produced, in both poetry
and prose, was this short descriptive verse which so vividly
evokes the feeling of winter.*

A wrinkled, crabbed man they picture thee,
Old Winter, with a rugged beard as grey
As the long moss upon the apple tree;
Blue lipt, an ice-drop at thy sharp blue nose;
Close muffled up, and on thy dreary way,
Plodding alone through sleet and drifting snows.

They should have drawn thee by the high-heapt hearth,
Old Winter! seated in thy great armed chair,
Watching the children at their Christmas mirth,
Or circled by them, as thy lips declare
Some merry jest, or tale of murder dire,
Or troubled spirit that disturbs the night,
Pausing at times to rouse the mouldering fire,
Or taste the old October brown and bright.

from

KINGHAM OLD AND NEW
W. Warde Fowler

*As well as a number of important works on nature and
wildlife, W. Warde Fowler also wrote about many aspects
of local history, including, in 1913, the story of his home
village of Kingham in Oxfordshire, from which these
wintry recollections are taken.*

We had two or three severe winters in the early
eighties: winters that were positively dangerous to
animal life, and especially so for the birds. I think it
was in the winter of 1884/85 that the fieldfares, and
to some extent the redwings, suffered most severely.
They became so weak that, shy as they are in general, they could hardly struggle out of reach of your
hand. I remember catching one and putting him in
my pocket to take home to revive, but while he was
still there his life slipped away.

But these winters never quite reached at any point
such a pitch of wintriness as we had already experienced in 1881. The night before the great storm I
spent at Kingham and had planned to go into Oxford
next day for a few hours to do some work. It was
blowing hard from the north-east, and there had been
snow in the night, but there was not enough to make

me change my mind; I was still young enough to enjoy wintry weather.

I took with me a few sandwiches, and a little whisky in a flask in case of accidents. I suppose I had a great-coat of some kind, but I had (and have) such a dislike for greatcoats that it was certainly a very light one.

In the train I met the Rector of Chadlington and his daughters who were going to London, and I remember that as we drew near Oxford he suddenly said, 'Is that drifting snow, or is it a blizzard?' I looked to the east and saw a cloud of powdery snow approaching the train; at the moment I thought it was only a drift, but it continued and increased, and we began to divine that we were going to have an unusual experience. However, I was intent on my work – what it was I have quite forgotten – and as I was to return by train at a quarter to four or so, I had no misgivings that I can remember.

The train reached Oxford without incident, and Fowler made his way to his college to continue with his work.

I was sitting in my room in college with a rug over my knees, when my old friend and schoolmaster, F.E. Thompson, dropped in on me, and we had some pleasant talk. Neither of us, as far as I can remember, was anxious about the chances of railway travel, but at that time, though the blizzard was declaring itself rapidly, it had not shown us what it could do in the way of drifts.

Later, when I made my way down to the station as it was growing dusk, I was hardly prepared to find that my train had been snowed up at Radley, and was not expected in Oxford that night.

The porters at Oxford assured me that the slow train, rather late, would be sent on, and that no fatal snow-drift had been reported towards Chipping Norton Junction. I therefore determined to take my chance: for if I went back to college I should find nothing to eat and no bed ready aired for me. The desire to be at home in such weather was strong in me, though I certainly had some doubt about getting there.

I was not alone, luckily, in my second-class carriage: I could have done with a whole carriage-full, packed like sardines, for warmth, for the cold was intense and the snow-powder was getting in between the joints of the window-frames.

Slowly, slowly we made our way over the waste of snow, stopping at every station and almost stopping at many another place where the snow came pouring over the eastern side of some cutting; and the soft velvety feeling of our progress was such as I have never experienced since.

What might be my fate at any moment I knew not, so long as we were at any distance from a station, and the most trying part was the long stretch of seven miles between Hanborough and Charlbury.

When at last we reached Charlbury station I felt great relief and was half inclined to get out. But again the longing for home got the better of me and I did not relish the prospect of being snowed up in the inn at Charlbury.

To cut short the story of this interminable journey, as it seemed, we ran safely into harbour at our own station somewhere about half-past-five.

So far so good: but my troubles were not yet over. No sooner than I had issued out into the road that in less than a mile of easy walking should have brought me to my own door, than I felt it impossible to go forward. I have never had this sensation since then, but I can feel it even now.

The north-east wind was in furious blast, straight upon my face, down the road, and had blown down the large strong sign of the Langston Arms Hotel which had then been lately built close to the station.

I pressed on, but only for a few steps: I became aware that I should lose my eyesight with the mad fury of the wind and the millions of particles of sting-ing snow. My eyes had been sore and tender lately, and I dared not risk them; my ears too, might be endangered, for they had long been amiss. So I turned and sought the shelter of the inn.

I was shown into a room with a tolerable fire, and some tea soon revived me. But that comfort soon passed away, and I began to feel the cold air breathing on me from every corner of the room as I sat before the fire.

I thought I would make another effort, paid my bill, and sallied out again. But in two minutes I was back there again, fairly beaten by the elements. There was nothing to do but wait and hope for a lull, and I

settled down again before the fire with such books as the hotel could produce. Two of them I remember well: Jules Verne's *From the Earth to the Moon*, which I read with avidity and delight, wishing indeed that the bottle of 'Nuits' were mine, with which they regaled themselves in the projectile. The second book was a handbook of medicine for the family.

When Jules Verne was exhausted, this other book struck in as a good second fiddle. I became gradually convinced that I had all the diseases about which it told me, in the same way as I had been convinced by Warren's *Diary of a Late Physician* at the tender age of eleven, that I was in an advanced stage of consumption when I read that one of its surest symptoms is a voracious appetite in the patient.

From these gruesome studies I was aroused by a sense of emptiness and rang for some supper, at the same time asking to see a bedroom where I might sleep. The supper I enjoyed, but the bedroom in the newly-built house smelt so chilly and draughty, that I decided to try that short mile home once more – if I could get anyone to try it with me.

By this time it was known in the station that I was imprisoned in the hotel, and I presently received a message from the goods foreman that he and another man were going up to Kingham and would take me in tow, and at the same time the landlord assured me that the storm was slightly abated.

At about ten o'clock the two men called for me. To protect my eyes from the wind, while we had to face it, I tied my handkerchief over them, and took the foreman's arm; the other man carried the lantern.

As the wind was a little less furious than it had been, we managed very well till we came to the cross-roads about a third of our way. The snow was not very deep here, as the wind sweeping in the same direction as the road had blown it down into the valley. But when we came to the sharp turn to the left, where the signpost is now, we found the snow drifted on the road up to the tops of the hedges, and we were forced to get into the field on the leeward side.

In this way we struggled along till we came to the railway bridge over the Chipping Norton line, and once over that – no easy task, for we had to get back into the road and the drifts – we thought we had laid the worst behind us.

But down in the flat meadows and the road across them, there was an even depth of soft snow into which we had to plunge up to our knees, and some-times deeper. It was here that I felt that desire, of which I had often read, to lie down in the snow and go to sleep, and with it the conviction that one more effort must be made and all would be well.

At last, though it took a long time, we were across the meadow and the brook, and mounting the hill to reach better shelter from the merciless wind.

I now remember no more till we stood at the door of my newly-built house, trying to rouse my house-keeper, Mrs Toon, who had given me up and gone to bed. At last she came, and I bade adieu to my kind and

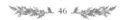

helpful companions. The last words I said to them (so Mrs Toon reminds me), were that I did not need any longer to hold my hat on as I had been doing, for it was frozen to my head!

I found that Mrs Toon and her boys had been working hard to keep the snow out of the house. The wind had somehow lifted a ventilator or trap-door and the snow had been pouring down the stairs. There was also a drift of it all the way from the front door to the back. But after a good warming by the kitchen fire, I went to bed and slept well, and the next morning I felt none the worse.

CHRISTMAS AT BROUGHTON CASTLE
THE LORD SAYE & SELE

Medieval Broughton Castle near Banbury, the moated home of Lord and Lady Saye & Sele, has been owned by the family for more than six centuries. Open to the public during the summer season, the castle contains much of historic and architectural interest, including a secret meeting-place used by the Parliamentarians during the Civil War. But it is the magnificent Great Hall which has been the traditional focal point at Christmastime, as the present Lord Saye & Sele recalls in these childhood memories.

Broughton Castle near Banbury, the medieval moated home of Lord and Lady Saye & Sele

Christmas when I was a child at Broughton revolved round the castle's Great Hall where there was always a roaring log fire and a large Christmas tree at one end. It was a real family occasion, and each year a number of relations – they always appeared to me to be elderly – came to stay with us.

Christmas dinner was a grand affair in those days. At half past seven the gong would be sounded, and everyone trooped off to dress for dinner. At 8 o'clock the gong sounded again and the party

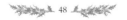

assembled in the Great Hall before filing into the Dining Room.

The dinner itself tended to be long-drawn-out, and indeed seemed to me at that time to be a rather tedious affair! But it was certainly enlivened by the decorations and the traditional Christmas fare, and especially by the arrival of the Christmas pudding aflame with brandy.

I can remember times when the winter weather was cold enough for the moat to be frozen, which added to the excitement of the festive season, for we were able to go skating, but I have no recollection of a Christmas when it actually snowed.

These festive occasions probably did not vary greatly from those in many other families, except of course that there was always the realisation that the Great Hall at Broughton had witnessed such seasonal celebrations for more than 600 Christmases.

from

VILLAGE SONG AND CULTURE
ᗰᴊɪᴄʜᴀᴇʟ Pɪᴄᴋᴇʀɪɴɢ

Michael Pickering based his 1982 study of the culture sur-
rounding traditional rural songs on the north Oxfordshire
village of Adderbury and its immediate neighbourhood.
Among the wealth of material he gleaned during his
lengthy researches, were several examples of Christmas
carols whose history was inextricably woven into vil-
lage life. They were sung mainly during the nineteenth
century, having been handed on by word of mouth from
generation to generation, and were part of a much wider
collection made in the early years of the present century by
one of the villagers, Janet Heatley Blunt. The following
extract from this fascinating study opens with a carol once
sung by local children on their rounds at Christmastime.

Now Christmas being come you see,
Let us rejoice and sing,
For great the news which can refuse
He did for sinners die.

So merry Christmas to you all,
It is a Christmas year.
So may you all, both great and small,
Enjoy your happy new year.

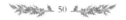

It is near two thousand years ago
Since carols first were sung.
The shepherds who were taught to do,
Joined by that heavenly throng.

It is true upon the cross he died,
No sinner can deny.
For great the news which can refuse
He did for sinners die.

So merry Christmas to you all,
It is a Christmas year.
So may you all, both great and small,
Enjoy your happy new year.

After they had sung and received their pennies (or, when at Adderbury House, 'a new shining sixpence' from the Misses Cawley), the children parted from the house they were visiting, with:

We wish you all a happy Christmas,
Happy Christmas, happy Christmas,
We wish you all a happy Christmas
And a bright new year when it comes.

Apart from the carol singing, Christmas was not a particularly special festival for children of working-class families in the village. The situation behind the blunt statement of one villager who grew up in the early part of this century, was replicated in many

The singing of Christmas carols by children is still a popular part of our seasonal celebrations, even if many of those who perpetuate the ritual are blissfully unaware of the old traditions from which the custom has evolved

cottage homes: 'I was one of a largish family, so there was nothing much to spare.'

At that time of year, the rich rather than the Lord provided: a dole of food, clothes or fuel for the poor, a dinner or a party for the old folk or children…

Christmas was certainly a holiday, but nothing like that associated with Banbury Fair and Club Day, when labourers' families came together again. Domestic reunions at Christmas before the first world war were a predominantly middle-class affair. One local carol expresses both the pleasure villagers took in the festival, and suggests the place it took in their year. This disparity between emotion and occasion seems to have been general for the country poor of the region.

During Christmas Day at Juniper Hill in the eighties, there 'was little visiting of neighbours and no family reunions, for the girls in service could not be spared at that season, and the few boys who had gone out in the world were mostly serving abroad in the army'. This reality is reflected in the song:

Sing we are merry,
Christmas is here.
Days that we loved best,
Days in the year,
Bring forth the holly,
The box and the bay
To deck out our cottage
For glad Christmas Day.

Sing we are merry,
Be of good cheer.
Talk of the absent
And wish they were here.
Sisters at service
And brothers away;
Oh how I wish
They were with us today.

Sing we are merry,
Sing of Christ's birth.
Sing what the angels sang:
Peace upon earth.
Parents and children
In white garments dressed,
Hasten to church
To sing praise with the rest.

*Michael Pickering also delved into the history of the
Adderbury Waits, whose contribution to the Christmas
celebrations was another facet of traditional village life.*

The occasion for the Adderbury Waits' singing was,
as with the children's May singing and the mummers'
performances, seasonal and perambulatory. The village
musicians, accompanied by the party of singers with
whom they made up the waits, performed outside
people's houses at Christmastime. One would imagine, because of the demands of their daytime work,
that this took place mainly during the evenings of the

Christmas season, though it is possible that Christmas Day itself, and maybe Boxing Day, were exceptions to the rule.

A villager whose songs were sung frequently by the Adderbury Waits was Thomas Hayward. Born in the latter half of the eighteenth century, he was for a time landlord of the Coach and Horses Inn, and a keen amateur musician who composed hymns for use in the parish church. One particular Christmas carol written and composed by Hayward and called 'Adderbury Church' was a special favourite:

All glory to God, and peace upon earth
Be published abroad at Jesus's birth;
The forfeited favour of heaven we find
Restor'd in a Saviour, the friend of mankind.

Our newly born King by faith we have seen,
And gratefully sing his goodness to men,
That all men may wonder at what we impart,
And joyfully ponder his love in our heart.

Then let us behold Messiah the Lord,
By prophets foretold, by angels adored.
Let every believer his mercy adore
And praise him for ever when time is no more.

*Another old carol sung by the Adderbury Waits was called
'Hark, Hark What News?' a title which familiarity and
local dialect corrupted to 'The Owd 'Ark 'Ark'. This was
also attributed to Thomas Hayward, although its origin is
less certain:*

Hark! Hark! What news the angels bring!
Glad tidings of a newborn king,
Born of a maiden, virgin pure,
Born without sin, from guilt secure.

Hail! Mighty prince, eternal king,
Let heaven and earth rejoice and sing.
Angels and man with one accord
Break forth in songs to praise the Lord.

May we contemplate and admire
And join with the celestial choir.
And tend our voices to the sky
All glory be to God on high.

from

PIT PAT, THE PAN'S HOT
Isabel Colquhoun

*The little village of Brightwell-cum-Sotwell, not far from
Wallingford, was Isabel Colquhoun's childhood home.
The happy years she spent there are recalled in* Pit Pat,
the Pan's Hot, *a fascinating account of a young life in
rural Edwardian England before 'progress' and two world
wars brought their irreversible change. She still lives in
the same locality – in Wallingford itself – and when she
wrote the book in 1975, she borrowed its title from an old
Shrove Tuesday carol once sung by the village children.
Her Christmas reminiscences, abridged here, bring back
all the happiness and innocence of the festive season seen
through a child's eyes in those early years of the century.*

Oh! those wonderful Christmases! As children,
we counted the days for weeks beforehand. But let
me hasten to add that Christmas was essentially a
Christian festival. Commercialism was not so rife. It
was, indeed, a season of goodwill.

Cottage housewives liked to begin their preparations about a month in advance. Many had paid a
small amount each week into a 'slate club', and the
share-out took place at about that time. How useful
that money would be to buy the extras required for

A wintry scene in about 1910 in Isabel Colquhoun's home town of Wallingford

the Christmas puddings and mincemeat, for women prided themselves on always making their own. Indeed, I do not remember seeing ready-made puddings or jars of mincemeat in the shops.

Of course the dried fruit did not come packed in cartons, already washed. It was bought loose, wrapped in blue paper shaped like a cone, and very much mixed up with grit. Much time had to be spent on cleaning it. First it was washed in two or three lots of water. Then it was spread out on a tin tray and dried, usually on top of the hob. Candied peel came in big pieces with large lumps of sugar clinging to it. How we loved to 'pinch' a piece of this while mother's back was turned, or while we were cutting it up into tiny particles!

Then the raisins had to be stoned, lovely dark brown, juicy, sticky raisins. What a job! We always had

a basin of water and a damp piece of rag on which to wipe our fingers constantly, as, with a knife, we slit open each raisin and got out the stones.

There was the suet to be grated (no packeted suet then), and the breadcrumbs to be made, the orange and lemon peel to grate and the juice to be extracted. How we loved the smell of all these preparations.

Lastly, mother would give us a few coppers to go to The Lion for a half-quarter of brandy for the mixing. Everyone present had to stir the pudding and make a wish. If funds allowed, one or two silver threepenny bits or sixpences were dropped in. Could we really wait until Christmas Day to taste all this?

I cannot remember much carol-singing in the village. I imagine this was because all the biggest houses worth visiting were on the outskirts, and with no street lighting, children were not tempted to go very far on the dark winter evenings, but you could count on a visit from the mummers some time before Christmas. You might get a warning by one of the party knocking and asking permission to come in and perform their play, but you might not. The door might have been flung open and in trooped the mummers, in very weird costumes usually made of wallpaper and with faces blacked all over. Once inside, without more ado, they began acting their play.

Naturally, the gentry went out of their way to be generous at Christmas, and to see that as far as possible no family was without a Christmas dinner, so every employer gave each of his employees a large piece of beef for the festive occasion. It was the custom of these farmers to go into Wallingford on the day of the Fat Stock Show, and there choose a whole carcase to be cut up into joints for their workmen.

The size and quality of the joint awarded to each employee was determined by both the size of his family and by his working position, so that a gardener or coachman could expect to have a primer cut than the cowman or farm labourer. At any rate, the chances were that no-one would be without a joint on Christmas Day.

The farmers themselves would enjoy the same meal of roast beef, for turkeys were not at all popular in those days, though a goose was sometimes fattened for the occasion. A few people who worked for themselves and so could not depend on an employer's generosity, fattened a cockerel or hen.

And so, with the home-made Christmas pudding and mincemeat, the roast beef, home-grown vegetables and a few extras like nuts, oranges, dates and figs bought with a few shillings carefully squeezed out of the housekeeping money, all was set for the meal of the year.

Christmas Day began early for most people, especially for the bell-ringers who liked to greet the day with a peal on the six bells of St Agatha's church.

At one time, my father was foreman of the ringers, and I recollect how, before he went to bed on Christmas Eve, he always left several pint bottles of beer on the kitchen table and left the door unlocked,

so that the first sounds I heard early on Christmas morning were two or three men calling in for a drink on their way to the belfry. Of course, this was at about 5.30 a.m. and dark at that, but this was the signal for me to reach down to the bottom of my bed to see if Father Christmas had really come and filled my stocking.

What a thrill of thrills to feel the stocking bulging with who knows what! I was supposed not to touch it until mother came in later on and gave me a light, but excitement and curiosity often proved too strong, and in the dark I emptied the contents and felt them to see what they were. Nothing very special of course, but they were priceless treasures to me.

Most stockings were filled with the same kind of presents: an orange, an apple, a few nuts, dates and figs, some sweets, perhaps a new handkerchief or a piece of new hair ribbon, a hair slide or an inexpensive brooch or bracelet, with often a halfpenny, penny or sixpence (what wealth!) in the toe. Simple things, but what delight they brought.

Children really believed in Father Christmas. I did, for years and years. I remember in particular one Christmas Eve night when it seemed I had been asleep for hours, I heard someone in my room and the rustling of paper. I shut my eyes even tighter. I dared not open them, lest I see the dear old man himself, or have my presents snatched away from under my very nose.

Later on, some of my older friends began to cast doubts on whether Father Christmas was real. Sad and disillusioned, I determined to prove it one way or the other.

Our staircase had a door at the bottom which led into the living room, so one Christmas Eve night I tried to stay awake and when I judged it to be the right time, I crept halfway down the stairs from where I could peep over the top of the door and see into the room. My dream was shattered. There at the table sat my mother and father filling my stocking. I can even recall hearing my father say, 'We'd better put something in the toe first', and there and then he fished into his pocket and produced a sixpence.

I crept back into bed. All the magic had gone. Never again would my bulging black stocking thrill me with joy. I continued to let my parents think that I still believed in Father Christmas for a few more years, but the joy had gone out of it and with it part of my childhood, and eventually I told them not to bother. I think they, too, were disappointed and saddened to think that I was growing up.

Most people tried to get to one of the services on Christmas Day. The churches were decked with evergreens and flowers, when and where possible. The oil lamps were well trimmed and the candles all aglow. A midnight service was unheard of.

Most domestic servants (having called their masters and mistresses) went to the 7 a.m. service so that they could get back in time to get fires going and breakfast ready while their 'betters' were at the 8 o'clock service. The 11 o'clock service was always well-attended.

Wives wanted their men out of the way while they cooked the meal of the year, so the church had its full complement of men, and of children who had to be compelled to tear themselves away from the contents of their stockings. The old church rang with the lusty singing of the old familiar carols – 'Hark the Herald', 'While Shepherds Watched', 'O Come All Ye Faithful'.

After church came the great moment – Christmas dinner. Would the beef be tender? Would the pudding turn out all right? Could a little spirit be spared to set it alight? Well, somehow everything came up to expectations. Then the washing-up was done, the fire stoked up in the front room (for those who had one) and the family settled down for the rest of the day.

There were the fruits and nuts to eat, any new toys to play with, the Christmas cards to look at again, though they were few in number compared with the hoards which come spilling through our letter-boxes nowadays. But there was all the more time to read, examine and comment on each one before it found its way to the mantelpiece where it stood until Twelfth Night among the holly and the ivy.

After such a sumptuous dinner, tea was rather *de trop*, and most of us could only manage just a cup of tea. We spent the evening playing simple card games, enjoying ourselves with Ludo or Snakes and Ladders, or we played Consequences. There was no radio or television, yet how we enjoyed those simple games, and when bed time came eventually, we felt, one and all, what a lovely Christmas Day it had been.

CHRISTMAS WITH SIR ROGER DE COVERLEY

Joseph Addison

*Another celebrated Oxford scholar was the essayist
and politician Joseph Addison (1672–1719), who was
instrumental in the founding of* The Tatler *and* The
Spectator. *It was in his contributions to the latter that
he wrote about the life of one of his best-known characters,
Sir Roger de Coverley. In these seasonal lines, Addison
describes Sir Roger's characteristically expansive mood at
Christmastime.*

Sir Roger, after the laudable custom of his ancestors,
always keeps open house at Christmas. I learned from
him that he had killed eight fat hogs for this season,
that he had dealt about his chines very liberally
amongst his neighbours, and that in particular he had
sent a string of hogs-puddings with a pack of cards to
every poor family in the parish.

I have often thought, says Sir Roger, it happens very
well that Christmas should fall out in the middle of
winter. It is the most dead uncomfortable time of the
year, when the poor people would suffer very much from
their poverty and cold, if they had not good cheer, warm
fires, and Christmas gambols to support them.

I love to rejoice their poor hearts at this season,
and to see the whole village merry in my great hall. I

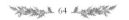

allow a double quantity of malt to my small beer, and set it a running for twelve days to every one that calls for it. I have always a piece of cold beef and a mince-pye upon the table, and am wonderfully pleased to see my tenants pass away a whole evening in playing their innocent tricks, and smutting one another.

I was very much delighted with the reflexion of my old friend, which carried so much goodness in it. He then launched out into the praise of the late act of parliament for securing the Church of England, and told me with great satisfaction, that he believed it already began to take effect, for that a rigid dissenter who chanced to dine at his house on Christmas Day, had been observed to eat very plentifully of his plumb-porridge.

GOODWILL TO MEN: GIVE US YOUR MONEY

Pam Ayres

The perceptive and often outrageously witty poems of Oxfordshire's own Pam Ayres have earned her wide fame. Her performances on television, radio and the stage, as well as on record, have delighted millions, and her books of verse have consistently been in the best-sellers' lists. There is virtually no subject immune from the unmistakable Pam Ayres' treatment, and Christmas is no exception, as these wryly humorous verses testify.

It was Christmas Eve on a Friday,
The shops was full of cheer,
With tinsel in the windows
And presents twice as dear.
A thousand Father Christmases
Sat in their little huts,
And folk was buying crackers
And folk was buying nuts.

All up and down the country,
Before the light was snuffed,
Turkeys they got murdered,
And cockerels they got stuffed.
Christmas cakes got marzipanned,
And puddin's they got steamed,

Pam Ayres: Christmas has not escaped her inimitable treatment

Mothers they got desperate,
And tired kiddies screamed.

Hundredweights of Christmas cards
Went flying through the post,
With first-class postage stamps on those
You had to flatter most.
Within a million kitchens

Mince pies was being made.
On everybody's radio,
'White Christmas', it was played.

Out in the frozen countryside,
Men crept round on their own,
Hacking off the holly
What other folks had grown.
Mistletoe in willow trees
Was by a man wrenched clear,
So he could kiss his neighbour's wife
He'd fancied all the year.

And out upon the hillside
Where the Christmas trees had stood,
All was completely barren
But for little stumps of wood.
The little trees that flourished
All the year were there no more,
But in a million houses
Dropped their needles on the floor.

And out of every cranny, cupboard,
Hiding place and nook,
Little bikes and kiddies' trikes
Were secretively took.
Yards of wrapping paper
Was rustled round about,
And bikes were wheeled to bedrooms
With the pedals sticking out.

Rolled up in Christmas paper,
The Action Men were tensed,
All ready for the morning
When their fighting life commenced.
With tommy guns and daggers
All clustered round about,
'Peace on Earth – Goodwill to Men',
The figures seemed to shout.

The church was standing empty,
The pub was standing packed,
There came a yell, 'Noel, Noel!'
And glasses they got cracked.
From up above the fireplace
Christmas cards began to fall,
And trodden on the floor, said:
'Merry Xmas to you all.'

from

THE STORY OF SWALCLIFFE
Dorothy G. M. Davison

In 1943 Dorothy Davison wrote a brief but fascinating
history of the little village of Swalcliffe, a few miles
to the west of Banbury. She included in it numerous
recollections of life in Swalcliffe Park, the former home
of the Norris family which today serves as a school.
Her account of the festive season at the house is typi-
cally evocative of a Victorian family Christmas in rural
Oxfordshire.

At Christmas there was sometimes a dance in the
kitchen. A story goes that on one occasion when the
room was very full, the little old fiddler was hoisted
on to the dresser where a chair had been placed, to
put him out of the way.

On Christmas Eve the waits or carol singers
came round. They called at every house in the village and they sang Christmas hymns, songs and carols.
The favourite one was 'How Beautiful Upon the
Mountains', but 'While Shepherds Watched' came
first, and 'Good King Wenceslas' followed on. One
man had a flute on which he sounded the preliminary
note. They sang in the front hall, where they were
very welcome.

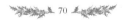

The family were all there to listen; even the grand-children, when they were small, were hauled from their beds as a great treat, wrapped in shawls. They enjoyed it, till the grandfather, with a secret smile on his face walked round and pressed a gold sovereign into the leader's hand and the choir disappeared through the green baize doors to begin again in the servants' hall.

As the children grew older they would hear the muffled peal of the church bells, and then, at midnight, the joyous clashing when the muffles came off. The sound of the bells seemed to vibrate in the tower and to crash through the windows of the green room, so that, coupled with the cold moonlight, hearing and vision became one with the feeling that it was glorious Christmas Day.

On Christmas morning the church was full, everyone sang and people looked happy. 'O Come All Ye Faithful' rang out year after year, while 'Glory to God in the Highest', as an anthem, seemed to reach the highest pinnacle of praise in the old church, with the organ pealing out and the choir singing, and the scarlet cloaks of the girls matching the berries of the holly entwined in the pillars about the pews.

At Christmastime there was generally a school treat or an entertainment at the school, when village performers would do their best to be amusing. Sometimes there would be a concert. A popular song was about 'Humphrey with his flail' and 'Dorothy Draggletail'. There were many songs, some with rousing choruses in which the audience would join in.

On Twelfth Day the decorations in the house were taken down, and after a service in the church (it being the feast of the Epiphany) the choir girls in their red cloaks, and hats alike, came up to the Park.

They were given drinks of steaming hot elder-berry wine made by the housekeeper who also kept the red cloaks in camphor during the summer. The girls stood round a table in the billiard room and Miss Mary Norris entertained them. She trained the choir of children and played the organ in the church. Her elder sisters, Ellie and Annie, taught in the Sunday School and sat with the boys and girls in church. Their father was known as the Squire and there was close co-operation between him and the vicar, the Reverend Canon Payne.

On Twelfth Day, too, the bell-ringers came to the Park. The bells were of bright pinkish copper. Six or eight men stood in a row, each man holding two bells, one in either hand, held by a clean new-looking leather strap. They played chimes, occasionally crashing all the bells together and beginning again.

On one occasion the ringers from Chacombe were invited to play at Swalcliffe Park together with the Swalcliffe ringers, when all of them were entertained.

Another Christmas jollity was the coming of the mummers. From a nursery window looking into the back yard, there was a tangled vision of black faces and men tumbling about in semi-darkness. But the children were snatched away from the window and were not allowed to look.

But later, when the mummers performed their play inside the house, a story seemed to emerge. It was told in primitive singsong verse by the men. There was some sort of a fight and a struggle and a man lay upon the floor. Someone fell upon him and pulled out a tooth which was held up for the audience to see; it was an immense one, probably a horse's tooth.

There was a doctor in a top hat and knee breeches; there was a man with a black face; another man wore a ragged petticoat and a woman's battered sun bonnet. The important part of the play seemed to be when the doctor took the hand of the man lying on the floor, pulled him up and shouted, 'Roise up King Jarge and foight again', then there were cheers all round and the play came gradually to an end.

Most of this was founded on ancient tradition, handed down from father to son over the ages. Unknown to most people, the play was based on folklore, on the worship of nature and on the conflict of good and evil.

THE BOAR'S HEAD AND OTHER STORIES

John Norton

There are many seasonal customs associated with
the Oxford colleges, some of very early origin. This
selection from the writings of John Norton begins with
the ancient ceremony of bringing in the boar's head
which still takes place at Queen's College at the start
of a traditional Christmas feast. It dates back to the
fourteenth century.

The traditional Boar's Head ceremony at Queen's College is probably one of the best-known seasonal junketings at the university. Preceding dinner, this ancient custom was originally held on Christmas Day, later being moved to Christmas Eve. Nowadays it takes place on a Saturday near Christmas.

Former members of the college are invited in turn as guests, and during the ceremony they stand at the side of the dining hall, with the Provost and Fellows behind the high table, facing the door through which the Boar's Head procession enters.

The head is decorated with gilded rosemary, bay leaves and holly, an orange is placed in its mouth, and it rests on a large silver platter which is carried into the hall with due ceremony by two men, escorted by the chef.

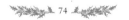

The ancient Boar's Head ceremony at Queen's College. This photograph was taken in 1957, but the ritual is unchanging

Heading the procession is the chief singer who sings the verses of the traditional Boar's Head Carol. Bringing up the rear is a group of choristers who sing the refrain between the verses.

On its way to the high table, the procession halts three times to allow each verse of the carol to be sung, until finally the boar's head is placed before the Provost who takes the orange from between the boar's teeth and hands it to the chief singer. The rosemary, bay and holly are also removed, and these are presented to the guests. After the ceremony is over, the whole company adjourns to another room for drinks, while the tables are rearranged for dinner.

This ancient festive custom is said to commemorate a resourceful scholar at Queen's College who came face to face with a wild boar while walking in the nearby forest of Shotover reading from the works of Aristotle. With great presence of mind – so the story goes – he thrust the book into the mouth of the ferocious beast, shouting as he did so, 'Swallow this if you can. It is in Greek!' The astonished boar promptly died, and the scholar survived to tell the tale. In another version of the story it is the boar itself which, having had the Aristotle thrust into its mouth, cries in protest, 'Graecum est' – this is in Greek – before expiring!

For those sceptics who prefer to think that the story is apocryphal, perhaps a more likely explanation for the boar's head ceremony is that it originated in the days when a large number of those studying at Queen's College, came from the far north of England

and were unable to make the long and arduous journey home for Christmas during the relatively short period of vacation. Instead they stayed in college and indulged themselves in an elaborate seasonal meal. In any event, a mid-winter feast involving a boar's head is said to have been a common practice in the north in medieval times, and so it is not unreasonable to suppose that the Queen's College students were quite happy to stay in Oxford for Christmas and perpetuate a custom with which they were already familiar.

Whatever the explanation, the Boar's Head ceremony at Queen's is a delightful tradition which, although not witnessed by the general public, has nevertheless become one of the highspots of the festive season in Oxford.

There are several different carols bearing the title 'The Boar's Head'. By tradition, it is the following version which is sung at the ancient Queen's College ceremony each Christmas.

The boar's head in hand bear I,
Bedecked with bays and rosemary;
And I pray you, my masters, be merry,
Quot estis in convivio.

The boar's head, as I understand,
Is the rarest dish in all this land,
Which thus bedecked with a gay garland,
Let us *servire cantico.*

Our steward hath provided this,
In honour of the king of bliss,
Which on this day to be serv-ed is,
In Reginensi atrio.

(Chorus between verses and at end)
Caput apri defero,
Reddens laudes Domino.

For non-classicists, the Latin lines in the three verses and
chorus above, are translated thus:

First verse: 'So many as are in the feast'.
Second verse: 'Let us serve with a song'.
Third verse: 'In the Queen's hall'.
Chorus: 'The boar's head I bring, giving praises to God'.

A much grander boar's head feast, by all accounts, was
that held each year at the Court of James I. On these
occasions a different Boar's Head Carol was sung, and it
was one being used in 1607 by the scholars of St John's
College, Oxford, at their own Christmas celebrations. The
following are its three verses.

The boar is dead,
Lo, here is his head,
What man could have done more
Than his head off to strike,
Meleager like,
And bringe it as I do before?

He livinge spoyled
Where good men toyled,
Which made King Ceres sorrye;
But now dead and drawne,
Is very good brawne,
And we have brought it for ye.
Then set down the swineyard,
The foe to the vineyard,
Let Bacchus crowne his fall,
Let this boar's head and mustard
Stand for pigg, goose and custard,
And so ye are welcome all.

The word 'swineyard' in the third verse is an allusion to the fact that the boar would have been the swineherd, or leader of the herd.

Drinking, of course, is inseparable from any feast, although these days it is difficult to name any one beverage which is synonymous with Christmas. In an age when supermarkets and off-licence retailers provide drinks in almost limitless variety, not only at Christmas but all the year round, there is little nowadays which can be described as typically seasonal, unless it is home-made hot punch.

This drink, with its multifarious recipes, was at one time widely accepted as the epitome of Christmas cheer, and one particular version was known by the unlikely name of Lamb's Wool. This consisted of warmed ale, numerous spices, eggs, cream, apples and sugar. It was usually made in considerable quantity to serve to the assembled guests at family parties and other festive gatherings.

Many of the great punch bowls once used for Lamb's Wool or similarly exotic beverages are still in existence, one of them at Jesus College, Oxford. This is an enormous silver-gilt affair made in 1726, measuring 19½ inches in diameter, which holds more than ten gallons. It is reputed to be the largest single piece of silver in Oxford. With it is an equally generous ladle capable of serving half a pint at a time.

Opportunities for these splendid utensils to be used for celebrating Christmas at Jesus College are, sadly, now rare, although in recent years they have come into their own again once a year on St David's Day. On these occasions, they figure in a revival of an old tradition in the Graduate Common Room, and are used to prepare and dispense a special punch known as 'swig'.

A traditional winter ceremony at which hot punch might well be served is one at All Souls' College. This is the 'Hunting the Mallard' custom which, strangely, takes place only once a century and was last repeated in 2001.

The mallard is the avian protector of All Souls' College, and the story goes that the bird in question flew out of a drainage ditch when the college foundations were being laid in the fifteenth century. It is still the subject of an intensive search on Mallard Night.

The search party, armed with torches, is made up of college Fellows, one of whom is given the title of Lord Mallard. This ceremonial leader is helped in his task by specially chosen attendants. Custom dictates that every corner of the college buildings is thoroughly searched – even the roof – to the rousing accompaniment of the traditional Mallard Song.

It seems that at one time it was an annual event associated with feasting, but it petered out during the eighteenth century. It was certainly back in full swing again by the beginning of the following century, although evidently not continuing on a yearly basis.

Records show that Mallard Night was always noted for its rowdiness, due to the gusto with which the participants sang the old song, and it is a matter of interesting speculation to ponder on how the Oxford of the early twenty-first century will react to the spirited proceedings when they next hunt the mallard at All Souls.

A no less bizarre seasonal custom is one which takes place on New Year's Day at Queen's College, a few days after the Boar's Head ceremony. This is the so-called 'Needle and Thread' tradition in which the Bursar gives the assembled guests a length of coloured silk threaded on to a needle, intoning as he does so: 'Take this and be thrifty'.

The needle and thread – or *aiguille et fil* in the French translation – is a pun on the name of Robert de Eglesfield, who founded Queen's College in 1340 and decreed that this curious custom should be enacted annually in his memory. His original intention was that the gift of a threaded needle, together with the accompanying instruction, should go to every member of the college, but as most students are away on 1 January, the recipients these days are confined mainly to specially invited guests.

ONCE UPON A TIME
HENRY CHAPPELL

Henry Chappell composed a considerable amount of poetry in the early years of the present century, and he wrote this Christmas poem especially for an Oxfordshire newspaper during the festive season in 1922. The introductory note which accompanied it described Chappell as 'the famous Great Western Railway poet', but in this verse he clearly forsook the frenetic world of locomotive boilers, steam traction and hot oil for a theme which is altogether more gentle and moralistic.

Once upon a time, in the long ago,
All on a Christmas Day,
A rich man's house was all aglow
And the feast was spread in goodly show,
When there came an old man out of the snow,
With a 'Gentles, shelter, pray!'

'I am old and poor, as you may see;
Yet do I not complain;
Let me but rest beside your fire,
The storm is wild and old limbs tire;
Trust an old minstrel with your lyre,
And he'll pay you with a strain.'

But, 'No', said my lady; my lord said 'No!'
And the guests did murmur loud
That such a one should front their sight,
A beggar, forsooth, on Christmas night!
So they sent him forth in the whirling white,
For aught they cared – his shroud.

A league, and he saw through a casement dim
A light amidst the storm.
The old man knocked, and the door ope'd wide,
And they drew him in to the turf fireside;
His hands they chafed, and his locks they dried,
And made him snug and warm.

With goat's flesh white, and barley bread,
They plied their aged guest,
And finished all, the old man spake,
'I bless you for the bread I break,
And blessed be all souls that take
A stranger in to rest.'
Then stood he up and clapped his hands,
Clapped one and two and three;
And lo! the walls grew high and white

With mistletoe and holly bright,
And shining, grew, bedecked with light,
A royal Christmas tree.

The children stood, all wonder-eyed,
Nor thought such bliss could be,
As one by one the stranger guest
Gave each the things they liked the best,
And, the more he gave the more possessed
The magic Christmas tree.

All night stayed he, the stranger guest,
And with the night he went;
Turned he his face toward the snow,
Then, 'One gift more, before I go,'
He said, and kissed the lintel low,
'I leave with you content.'

This is a tale of a Christmas time,
All in the long ago;
But bright eyes watch for the gifts today
That will dim with tears if we say them nay,
Nor magic tree will come their way
Unless we make it grow!

GHOULIES AND GHOSTIES
Mollie Harris

*Through her many books, articles and talks,
Oxfordshire writer and broadcaster Mollie Harris, who
lived in the village of Eynsham, delighted thousands
with her inimitable commentaries on the countryside
and her evocative reminiscences of the rural way of
life in years gone by. She was equally well known for
her regular contributions to the BBC's long-running
'everyday story of countryfolk',* The Archers, *in
which she played the part of Martha Woodford. She
penned these seasonal thoughts of the supernatural at
Christmastime in 1966.*

From ghoulies and ghosties and long-leggety beast-
ies and things that go bump in the night, Good Lord
deliver us.

Scottish prayer

When the mists of winter lie low over the meadows,
shrouding the countryside in a mysterious veil, one's
imagination can run riot and it is quite easy to slip
into the world of ghosts and things that go bump in
the night.

Hardly any village is without its pet ghost, and
my own village of Eynsham is no exception. Some
time ago a lady died here. She had lived in the same

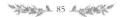

cottage for at least forty years and had been on friendly terms with the ghost of a monk who haunted her home. The cottage is situated quite near to where a huge Benedictine abbey once stood.

Relatives of a family who once owned the property, tell of the time when alterations were being made there. Flagstones were being removed in a place they called the dairy, and underneath them the workmen found the skeleton of a man. Whether these remains, and the friendly ghost which has haunted the cottage for generations, have any connection we shall never really know, but the lady who died there certainly thought so.

At nearby Stanton Harcourt there is a ghost story associated with the Manor House and Pope's tower. The ghost that once walked there was said to be Alice Harcourt, who met her death at the hands of the chaplain. The spirit of this unfortunate lady was supposed to have wandered backwards and forwards from the chapel to one of the fish ponds known as Lady's Pool, and in times of drought, when the water was low, her troubled spirit would be heard moaning and crying. But it is heard no more; her ghost was successfully 'laid' some years ago.

Again from Stanton Harcourt comes another story of the supernatural going back nearly two hundred years when a family by the name of Hall lived at Manor Farm.

Mr Hall was in the habit of going to the Harcourt Arms Inn more often than his wife liked, and at last

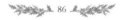

she found out that he actually went to visit the land-lady, a Mrs Surman.

Mrs Hall expostulated with her husband, but to no avail, and after some time she took a strong dose of poison. She was seen to go to the pump in the yard and rinse out the glass before she fell down dead.

After her burial, she 'came again' and walked round the farmyard and garden, and also round the inn where her rival lived. She was last laid in a pond which they say never runs dry. If it did, her ghost would walk again.

From records in the last century comes the story of a wager that was won by a village simpleton in 1894, and here I quote: 'At Shipton-under-Wychwood church there is a kind of bone house or hole where bones that were dug up in the churchyard have been put from time out of mind. In the village many years back, there was a man who others thought to be daft, or at least not so sharp as he should be. He was challenged one night at the public house that he dared not to go to the bone house at twelve o'clock at night and bring away a skull. The challenge was accepted, and on a given night he started off. Two of the men were to go to see that he did the job, and they hid them-selves in the bone house. At the stroke of twelve the man entered and took up a head, when a voice said: "Put that down it's mine." He did put it down and took up another, when the voice said again: "Put that down, it's mine." This time the man replied:

"What? Do you have two heads? Then I'll have one of them." And he won his wager.'

Most villages, especially those which skirt the Wychwood Forest, tell of ghostly coaches driven at a fantastic speed through the darkness, with headless drivers and with horses breathing fire from their nostrils. I have even heard that one has been seen here at Eynsham, but I've never had the pleasure of witnessing it.

One elderly man from the Burford area used to tell of a dark winter night when he was walking home along the Chipping Norton to Burford road. He was passing by Sarsden Pillars when quite suddenly a man came up alongside him. For a while the mysterious stranger walked and talked. Then from a nearby cottage a woman came out carrying a lantern, in the dim light of which the man from Burford saw his companion, whose head was neatly tucked under his arm. As soon as the stranger realised that he had been seen, he disappeared.

Our cottage is haunted. We had been living here for about three years, and during that time had heard queer noises. The family said it was the building contracting as the noises were mostly heard at night when the house was getting cooler. But the loudest noise was heard regularly at 6.45 p.m.

I happened to mention to a neighbour who had always lived in the village that we heard things in our cottage, and she calmly said: 'Well, you know who that is, don't you? That's Natty – Natty Gibbons. He was a baker who lived here years ago, a pale shy man who kept a pet fox.'

After that, Natty got blamed for all sorts of things, like leaving the doors and windows open, and each evening when the loud noise was heard, somebody was sure to remark that Natty had jumped out of bed with his boots on, or something just as silly.

Some years ago, however, my daughter-in-law was sitting in the lounge one evening sewing, and our dog lay sleeping beside her. Suddenly the dog woke, stood up stiffly with every hair down his backbone standing on end, and his tail out straight. His eyes travelled across the room and towards the stairs, and he made a quiet whining noise. Then my daughter-in-law heard a loud 'clump'. She ran out into the garden white and shaking. The time was exactly 6.45 p.m. but she knew nothing of our ghost at that time and was horrified when we explained the 'noise' she had heard.

A WEATHER EYE ON CHRISTMAS
Ian Fox

*The festive season, so we are constantly reminded, is
not what it used to be. Television, extended holidays,
relative affluence and rampant commercialism may tend
to dominate our modern Christmases, but the occasion
was celebrated with no less enthusiasm in years gone by.
When journalist Ian Fox wrote this account, he delved
into the archives of the erstwhile* Oxford Journal
Illustrated *for the period from 1909 to the 1920s to see
what was making headline news in Oxford all those
Christmases ago.*

The weather has always been a fruitful topic of conversation among the English, but it is only when we
suffer its more alarming excesses such as drought,
hurricane or persistent snow, that it merits coverage
in our newspapers today.

But in the early years of the century there was
little excuse needed for the columnists of the time to
indulge in detailed commentaries on even the most
normal of weather patterns. If it was seasonably cold,
it deserved comment; if it was unseasonably mild the
column inches were no less numerous.

In 1909, for instance, the citizens of Oxford were
being eloquently informed of the undoubted benefits
of a fine but cold Christmas week:

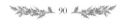

'There is, after all, some hope that this may prove a seasonable Christmas. It is a matter of real importance that it should be so. There is no class in the community that would not be the better and the happier for a fine Christmas week. The tradesmen will take much more money if fine, bright days tempt people forth for shopping. There will be a bigger run on the butchers' and poulterers' shops if appetite is promoted by brisk weather entailing vigorous exercise. Then there are the numerous travellers returning home for the season; how great a difference fine weather makes to them! Then the sportsmen, all but the foxhunters – and they have no objection to a week off – would like a good frost, drying up the rides for the covert-shooting and bringing in the snipe and wild duck. The children, also, are keen on skating, but it is too much to hope that the real ice will bear by Christmas time; however, the maple-wood floor always bears, and roller skates will be in great request during the Christmas holidays.'

The climate that year did eventually prove acceptable, and a few days after Christmas it merited a further report by a contributor described rather delightfully as 'an Oxford lady':

'The weather on the whole behaved satisfactorily for the Christmas holidays. It was more like a chilly April melting into November than a Christmas card winter…'

The mention of Christmas cards clearly gave the 'Oxford lady' a timely opportunity to inform her readers of one of her seasonal bones of contention:

Even the excesses of the winter weather in the early years of this century could not match the great freeze of 1895, when the Thames at Oxford was frozen over

'The majority of fashionable Christmas cards, it seems to me, are too large for ordinary envelopes, or so I found when I was getting my selection ready for post. When I sent round in haste to the nearest stationer's for a packet of mixed envelopes for Christmas cards, meaning envelopes larger than the ordinary size, such as I have usually bought to supply such deficiencies, the packet forthcoming had only two envelopes as large as an ordinary square envelope, and all the rest infinitely smaller. I went round to the stationer's in great wrath, and said I wanted envelopes for Christmas cards and not for dolls' notepaper, whereupon the lady stationer replied with dignity that the envelopes were arranged to fit *their* Christmas cards, and I felt crushed.'

One can only hope that the 'Oxford lady' eventually found satisfaction.

The following year the weather again received prominence, thanks once more to the assiduous attention still being paid to it by that same 'Oxford lady': 'Short of ice and snow, which is more agreeable in sentimental theory than in reality,' she maintained, 'sunshine is the best thing we can get for Christmas Day, and this year we had no lack of bright sunshine, with an exquisitely blue sky, for some hours. So one important accessory of a happy Christmas was assured. Snow and frost, though picturesque, are not very comfortable in this country, because we are not properly equipped for them, and a fine, dry, sunny

Such was the thickness of the ice on the Thames in 1895 that a coach and four – as well as a large crowd of incredulous Oxford townsfolk – gathered in the middle of the river

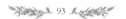

day is all that we can desire. The sunshine on Port Meadow made a beautiful picture, and in spite of a rather sharp wind – in fact, because of it – it was a delight to be out of doors.'

But apart from the weather, it was the profound subject of 'Christmas dietetics' which also made the headlines that year: 'Physiology has long taught the advantages of simplicity in dietetic matters,' stated the writer with suitable gravity, 'and its warnings may well be borne in mind during the festive season. All that counts for enjoyment is not condemned by physiology, for, as is well known, the appreciation of food contributes largely to its due appropriation for the bodily needs. The Christmas dinner, which is a highly cherished institution, is, after all, a simple affair, and its ingredients are in general of the most wholesome kind. Why do humorists persistently represent the opposite view? Roast beef or turkey and plum pudding represent in plain terms the constituents of what is from a physiological point of view a complete diet, presenting all classes of reparative material demanded by the great processes of nutrition. It contains a balance of proteins, fats, carbohydrates and mineral salts which go to make a healthy tissue. The plum pudding, in particular, is a complete food in itself, and the only risk of the Christmas meal is taking an excess of the good things which it provides.'

Any latent feelings of anxiety among readers were thus laid instantly to rest, except presumably for those guilty of 'taking an excess of the good things'.

Readers were also informed rather intriguingly that 'in Oxford, fortunately, the Christmastide festivities have not been marred by any calamitous happenings such as have saddened the homes of many people in one or two other parts of the country'.

What exactly these 'calamitous happenings' were, was left to the imagination, but at least Oxford did not suffer them. 'Here,' the report continued, 'favoured with comparatively fine weather' (the weather again) 'the Christmas season has been a time of family rejoicing, of happy reunions of parents with children who are now seeking their fortunes in other parts of the country, and in some instances in other parts of the world. There seems to have been no diminution of seasonable greetings and good wishes through the post. Oxford's Christmas may be said to have been a tranquil, and in most cases a pleasurable one, though some young people probably wished there had been a sharp frost last week to enable them to take advantage of the opportunity for skating upon the extensive floods.'

These 'extensive floods' were apparently the result of heavy rain which had fallen well before Christmas, and one group of citizens who were happily immune from their effects were the patients in the Radcliffe Infirmary where 'the medical and nursing staff always endeavour to make the lot of those whose misfortune it is to be in the institution at Christmastime as happy and joyous as possible, and many there are who no doubt will be able to say they spent a bright and happy Christmas in the Infirmary'.

In Christmas week the following year it was the turn of Oxford's shopkeepers to receive a seasonal mention:

'While from a spectacular point of view the drapers' establishments, stationers and toy shops, with their gayly decked windows, naturally come first for attractiveness at this season, the most unobservant person must realise during this week that the purveyors of meat, game and provisions have taken especial pains to demonstrate the fact that the Christmas dinner table, as well as the children's party, has to be provided for. At the premises of the principal butchers there are now to be seen first-rate displays of meat, purchased at the local and district fat stock shows, while at the fruiterers' shops, the rows of turkeys, geese and poultry on view, show what an abundance of prime birds are this year available. The windows of the fruiterers' shops, too, are quite alluring, and the florists have a plentiful supply of holly and mistletoe.'

The fact that fruiterers' shops were selling turkeys, geese and poultry must have been a perfectly normal practice back in 1911.

Preoccupation with the seasonal attractiveness of Oxford's shops, however, was not sufficient reason to exclude a somewhat churlish weather note:

'Owing to the weather, this has been essentially an indoor Christmas in every sense of the term, and even if the air had been bright and clear and frosty, the outdoor attractions in Oxford would hardly have proved a great draw.'

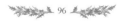

By 1913 Oxford was apparently just beginning to experience the first signs of traffic congestion:

'What with the Christmas shopping and the outbreak of motorbuses, the busy thoroughfares have been quite a peril these last few days. The great difficulty for those on foot is to get across the roads. There are, however, alleviations. Father Christmas with his crowd of small followers is as much in evidence as he has been in other years. The shops have eclipsed themselves in gaiety and fascination, and it is to be hoped that with so many attractions for the spending of money, everybody will get everything they want without being ruined in the process. Christmas comes but once a year, so we must make the most of it even if we are ruined.'

Helping to 'make the most of it' that year was a recipe for a Christmas cake, published somewhat belatedly on Christmas Eve and contributed by one Barbara Bocardo. It was a splendid affair requiring all manner of exotic ingredients, and it is to be hoped that Barbara Bocardo was not entirely unaware of the stern message in that 'Christmas dietetics' article published three years earlier.

Anyway, the following week, when it was all over, what better and more familiar subject was there to write about than the weather:

'Christmas seems to have been celebrated with much happiness and success generally, judging from the crowds in the churches and the people in the streets. The weather, perhaps, left something to be desired, but after our experience of last year, most of us were thankful there was nothing worse than a cold, wet wind.'

For good measure, the same columnist took the opportunity to make some timely comments about Oxford's public transport:

'The quiet of the main thoroughfares on Christmas Day, with neither trams nor buses running, even in the latter part of the day, carried us back to a time which is only a dim memory to the elderly, when Oxford was horrified at the prospect of widening Magdalen Bridge for the sake of the trams which were to cross it. It must have been almost as agitating as the present situation before Mr Morris brought things to a climax with his motorbuses. Why, by the way, if motorbuses must be the height they are from the ground, do not the builders put three steps instead of two?' Why not, indeed?

By the following Christmas, the First World War had started, and the gravity of the situation not surprisingly tempered the reporting of the city's festive events:

'The customary seasonal celebrations were observed in Oxford this year, but the festival, coming in the midst of war, was perhaps hardly celebrated in the same spirit as usual. In Oxford, as elsewhere, the loss of a relative had to be mourned by many a family. To such homes, Christmas had brought sorrow. But in others, soldiers were welcomed home from the training centres – and in a few cases even from the

Snow and frost transform the Thames towpath near Oxford into a winter wonderland

battlefields – to spend their Christmas leave. The outstanding feature of the celebrations in Oxford was the eagerness displayed, by rich and poor alike, to make Christmas a time of happiness and enjoyment for the wounded soldiers and the men of Kitchener's army now in the city.'

It was obviously a traumatic time, and with so much to report, there was not even a passing reference to the weather. But so important an omission was not allowed to remain for long, and by 1916, despite the stories of war, the topic had resumed its place in the Christmas reporting:

'The weather was favourable for outdoor exercise, and people generally seemed to be spending as happy a time as the conditions under which we are

living would permit. A quiet celebration of the great festival which is emblematic of peace and goodwill – strangely anomalous terms in these days – included the time-honoured features with which we are familiar, as well as the less familiar ones connected with the care of wounded soldiers.'

Peace had returned again by Christmas 1918, and there was an important carol-singing concert to review. Even this included the inevitable weather report:

'An enjoyable hour-and-a-half was spent on Sunday afternoon by an audience which filled the Sheldonian Theatre, listening to and taking part in the singing of Christmas carols under Professor Allen's genial instruction and guidance. His injunction not to regard the weather – which was very wet and unpleasant – but to make the occasion a happy gathering at which they were all going to enjoy themselves, at once removed all formality.'

A year later the Christmas weather really did give them something worth writing about, and they made the most of it:

'The Christmas of 1919 – the second since the armistice – may truthfully be described as one of the wettest on record. Rain fell every day from Christmas Eve to Sunday, and was particularly heavy both on Christmas Day and Bank Holiday. For this reason it was largely a "home" festival, family gatherings being a feature of the holiday. The church services did not seem to be so well attended as twelve months ago. Then the armistice had only just been signed, and people not in the habit of attending church regularly, felt it was a duty that was demanded of them. This year the weather probably kept many away who would otherwise have been present.'

The problem of declining church congregations was evidently the cause of some editorial concern, and in 1921 an eloquently worded reassessment of the Christmas festival was thought desirable in an increasingly materialistic world. The style of prose, quite normal in those days, would no doubt raise more than a few eyebrows among the newspaper readers of today:

'There is no festival in all the world like Christmas – the time when kindliness is the dominant characteristic of humanity, and happiness abounds. Easter is a day of rejoicing too, but it is not like Christmas. It represents triumph – victory over death – and its very joyousness is the reaction of sorrow. Christmas brings with it a childish spontaneity of happiness, a faith that sees no sorrow, that recognises goodness and ignores for a moment all blackness, all horror. It is called the children's festival but its name carries with it a double meaning. It is the time when men and women forget the present and live in the past, putting off their armour of suspicion, hard-headedness and selfishness, looking at life once more through rose-coloured spectacles, because they have, for a moment, the child-like soul.' Meaty stuff indeed for a newspaper.

Twelve months later, readers were evidently thought to be in need of a little guidance in choosing presents.

Christmas shopping seems to have been an exercise which deserved to be taken with extreme seriousness:

'To most of us the difficult, but certainly exhilarating task of choosing Christmas presents is the principal delight of the Yuletide season. It occupies our sleeping and our waking thoughts because it is something of an enigma. Possibly half the difficulties would vanish if we could pretend we do not know what things our relations have already, and if we decide to give them something that we should really enjoy buying, and not something we imagine ought to suit them. It is this dutiful habit of giving things supposed to be practical that makes the exchange of presents often an almost joyless thing between relations. There are so many things a girl might give her mother. Any item of dress, for example, is never out of place – a blouse, a hat, some item of underclothing that will spare her needle, a pair of slippers, a jumper, or, if these things are too expensive, a really nice pair of gloves.

'Menfolk, most difficult of all, never hope for very original gifts. A pair of slippers, a box of cigars, a pipe, or a bottle of whisky, are among the only things one can think of for father. While brothers – and other people's brothers – can expect silk handkerchiefs, ties, socks, cigarette holders and cases. A pair of fur gloves is, perhaps, a more uncommon gift, while one can sometimes fall back on a suitcase or a set of brushes.'

Good advice seems to have been the order of the day during that particular Christmas week. Having

dealt with present-giving, the paper turned its attention to entertaining and the duties of a hostess:

'Of all the people in the world, the Christmas hostess requires tact,' stated the writer knowingly. 'Her lot is not altogether an enviable one, although most of us admit the delights that come from throwing open one's house to visitors, of entertaining young and old with the lavish hospitality that is a feature of the season. The main difficulty of the Christmas hostess is in keeping a calm exterior. How can a woman be certain that her cook – if she is lucky enough to have one – will not burn the turkey, or, if all the cooking falls to her own lot, that she will not disgrace herself in some way through an uncertain oven? This is only one of a thousand worries that beset the hostess. Her charms must be in no-wise marred by these worries. Rather must she laugh with the merriest and, keeping these domestic duties at the back of her mind, fulfill the role of hostess with all the joie de vivre of which her personality is capable. The successful Christmas hostess is, above all things, a woman of tact and common sense.'

One cannot help wondering how many women in the Oxford of 1922 were able to heed the advice so freely offered, and actually performed their onerous Christmas duties in so thorough a manner.

Christmas came and went, however, and when it was assessed afterwards, true to form, the weather came into the reckoning:

'As was predicted, it was a fireside Christmas, the weather on Christmas Day, Monday, being such as to make the fireside the best place. All day Saturday the city was a hive of traffic, and the number of shoppers must have approached a record, even though, in some parts, tradesmen were heard to say that money was a trifle scarce.

'From outward appearances money did not seem to be scarce, and, in many instances, women home-ward bound wanted something far more spacious than the ordinary bus to hold their purchases. There was a huge demand for holly wreaths, but at times the prices for flowers assumed alarming proportions, at one place 2s 9d being asked for half-a-dozen small bronze-coloured chrysanthemums, while at another the assistant asked half-a-crown, and when told it was exorbitant, allowed a bunch of eight to go for eighteen pence.'

After divulging an act of such reckless generosity on the part of one Oxford shopgirl (who, one hopes, was not dismissed for showing a blatant disregard for her employer's profits), the report reverted once again to much more familiar ground: 'During Saturday the weather remained fine, but very cold. Sunday opened cold and dreary, but before lunch drabness had given way to sunshine. The afternoon was cold and very few people were out.'

It was seasonal cakes which earned special cover-age the following year, and the advice given, a week before Christmas, was clearly aimed at Oxford's more

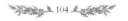

'The most unobservant person must realise that the purveyors of meat, game and provisions have taken especial pains to demonstrate the fact that the Christmas dinner table has to be provided for…'

indolent women judging by the opening lines: 'The housewife who lives by rule and regulation has already iced, as well as made, her Christmas cake, but, as many people in these days live more by their own sweet will than by rules and regulations, there are many who have made but not yet decorated their cakes…'

The next year it was apparently thought opportune during Christmas week to reiterate some of the basic tenets of the Christian festival, presumably for the benefit of those who had no idea what it was all

about or who had missed earlier instalments. If the subject-matter and style of prose appear today to be better suited to the pulpit than a newspaper, no such inhibitions evidently existed in 1924:

'Christmas is the most remarkable festival for many reasons. It reflects our delight in keeping birthdays, and it marks the human tendency to rejoice even more over the birth of the Little Lord than over His later triumph over death. Because of this worship and remembrance of a child, it has been called the children's festival – and yet it is for all, and not one section of the community, though it undoubtedly brings men and women back to childish hopes and simple kindliness and joyousness as no other festival does in the year.'

Meanwhile, back in the harsh world of commerce, prices were being quoted for some of the seasonal fare which Oxford folk would be buying that Christmas. 'There is every likelihood that the price of nuts will remain about the same,' said the report reassuringly, 'though there will be a tendency for the price of oranges and mandarines to increase.' Jamaican bananas, on the other hand, were quite modestly priced at 1½d a pound, although 2d was being asked for those from the Canaries. Turnips, carrots and parsnips were all listed at 1½d a pound, cauliflowers cost from 6d to 8p depending on size, and you could buy a pound of Egyptian dates for 6d. Artichokes were good value at 2d a pound, and for the same price you could buy a pound of Spanish onions.

However, 'owing to the foggy weather' fish was apparently scarce and was likely to cost between 2d and 3d a pound more than usual. But for a real treat – for those who could not afford a festive turkey or goose – English hares were described as 'cheap' and could be bought for 4s each, a considerable saving on a chicken or duck which would have cost at least 5s. For those with money to spend, the Christmas appetites in Oxford in 1924 were going to be well satisfied.

By 31 December it was all over once again, and that week's paper carried the usual report – weather commentary and all – on how the city had celebrated: 'Everywhere there was the festive spirit, notwithstanding the unpleasant weather which on Christmas Eve was dark and dismal, with torrential rain, relieved by bright sunshine for a few minutes, flashing lightning, loud peals of thunder, and a storm with hailstones as large as marbles.' Regrettably, the report added, 'there appeared to be an absence of carol-singers'. With that sort of weather it was hardly surprising.

'Fruit dishes for Christmas parties' was one of the seasonal items which grabbed the attention of readers the following year. The column led with a recipe for Orange Surprise, and offered numerous other fruity delicacies including an exotic concoction described as 'Pears à la Ricardo'. To ensure that readers were left in no doubt as to the contributor's culinary authenticity, they were informed that she was a First-Class Triple Honours Diplomee of the National Training School for Cookery in London. With such impressive credentials, her Orange Surprise or Pears à la Ricardo could hardly be ignored.

Christmas in Oxford in 1926 must have been a relatively uneventful affair as it was described as 'a sober holiday', despite the fact that 'licensed premises had an extension on Christmas Eve'. Two people were, however, arrested for drunkenness, one of whom was a hawker named Julia Birt 'of no fixed abode' who admitted that she did get drunk in St Aldate's Street on Christmas night. It was a certain Police Constable Rymills who had the job of terminating Julia's celebrations:

'He was at the Police Station when someone complained that she was entertaining the neighbourhood with songs which suggested that she had had "one two many". He left the Police Station, and as he turned the corner of Blue Boar Street he found the woman in a merry mood sitting on a seat outside the Town Hall, almost beneath the window of the Mayor's Parlour. Singing at the top of her voice, she annoyed the whole neighbourhood. Convinced that she had imbibed very freely, and equally convinced that her singing was not appreciated by anyone, he took her to the Police Station where, on recovery, she was allowed bail. But following this, there was another tale to tell – she got drunk again.'

For Julia Birt, Christmas in Oxford in 1926 was obviously a very merry one indeed – and the account of her celebratory exploits did not even mention the weather once.

from

LIFTING THE LATCH

Sheila Stewart

Mont Abbott, farm hand, labourer and shepherd, spent almost eighty years of his long life on the land around the Oxfordshire village of Enstone. In the 1980s, Sheila Stewart persuaded him to tell his life story, and it took her two years to transform the wealth of material she had collected on more than fifty tapes, into a remarkable biography which she called Lifting the Latch. *As far as possible, she faithfully reproduced Mont's own words in his warm Oxfordshire dialect, and in this first extract from some of his Christmas reminiscences, he recalls with affection his old friend Owen Reagan, landlord of Enstone's Harrow Inn, and a seasonal visit to nearby Heythrop House.*

Owen Reagan's log fires in the smoke-room and the tap-room were like him, roaring, generous, with great trunks stuck out into the room. He had huge hands with tremendous strength in his fingers. It were quite a sight to see a foaming gallon of beer, four pints in each hand, ascending from the cellar, followed by the rest of the giant Owen.

He'd warn any troublemaker only once, 'Sup up and get up.' Any further trouble, they huge hands 'ud

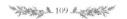

swoop like grabs and lift the startled offender in one almighty chuck, up six steps and into the street.

The best Christmas we ever had as children were thanks to Owen. I were a starving bwoy of ten before the first world war. We was still feeling the pinch badly at home. Owen asked Dad if I could go up to the mansion at Heythrop on Christmas morning to accompany his wife back home through the forest. Mrs Reagan were a good cook, and whenever the Brasseys had more guests than their chef could cope with, he'd send word to Owen for her to come and give him a hand.

It were another world up there. Everything were done on the grand scale, with an army of servants and workmen. The stables and coach houses was that posh and employed such a multitude, the stud groom were allowed to run his own pub on the premises.

There were a team to man the gas house where they made all their own fuel to light the mansion; and a bothy, a sort of hostel, where all the under-gardeners lived. There was several head gardeners, toffed-up to the nines like lords, holding sway over their 'ticular territories – the glasshouses, the mile-long borders of fantastical plants, the nuttery, the bowling green, the croquet lawn.

There was two lakes, one cascading into the other, where perch 'ud gather in a herd in the summer, and men 'ud gather in a barge in the winter to collect the ice to build the ice-rick which supplied the ice to make ice-cream and cool the wine.

Heythrop House hosts a meet of the Heythrop Hunt. It was here that
Mont Abbot was given half a cooked ham and other Christmas fare, as a
reward for sweeping the snow from the mansion's steps

Mrs Brassey retained a trained nurse full time
for the parish, and bought every bwoy a new pair
of boots and every gal a new warm cloak every
Christmas. Them Heythrop Red Riding Hoods was
the envy of every little gal in Enstone parish; and
the boots 'ud 'ave been a godsend, especially that
Christmas, in our family.

I crept inside the back portal to wait for Mrs
Reagan. The chef were Italian; hadn't a word of
English. He were like a tight round bomb about to
go off through his high hat at any moment. He tasted
everything, rolling his eyes, smacking his lips, flashing
his big white teeth, flinging his arms about, jabbering off the top of his head, swivelling on his heels,

Heavy snow at Chipping Norton in the 1920s. It was on a day such as this that Mont Abbot was to have met his ill-fated Kate to buy her a wedding ring at the local jeweller

and darting off in all directions for further flavours. His hands were podgy, yet swift and nimble. He had a wicked knife, and a clanging steel hung from hooks on his broad leather belt, and with these he ruled supreme. I were terrified of him at first. I could see him chopping up little bwoys into puppy-dogs' tails and relishing 'em like nobody's business.

Mrs Reagan warn't quite ready. A butler chap asked me if I'd like to earn a bob or two sweeping the snow off the front door steps. The chef yells at me, jabbering in Italian. I couldn't understand a word but I got the gist. I were to come straight back to the kitchen when I'd finished.

I had a job to fathom which were the front door steps; the mansion were built to face equally posh in all four directions. I done 'em all. It were biting cold and the soles of me boots warn't all that special, but us got over it. The butler chap were that pleased at the way I done 'em, he give me *fifteen* bob. And when he showed the chef my work, *he* loaded me up with two brown paper carrier bags stuffed with apples and pears, nuts and oranges, and half a cooked ham. I were a laden godsend that Christmas to our Mam, eking out her one rabbit.

Later in Mont's life story, he recalls one of the most
poignant of all his many memories. It was a bitterly cold
winter, and he was now engaged to his beloved Kate
Carey, a nurse at Oxford's Radcliffe Infirmary. In this
episode he refers to the Dovecot, which was his home, and
to the Litchfield, which was one of Enstone's inns.

I were going to bike to Chipping Norton to meet Kate off the early afternoon train, and we was going to Simms's, the jewellers on the Horsefair, to fit her wedding ring. It were the first half-day she'd had since before Christmas. They were always overworked at the Infirmary at this time of the year. There were plenty of flu about, but not so dangerous as in 1918.

On Saturday, first thing in the morning, it seemed quite mild as I opened the door of the Dovecot and wended my way in the dark down to the privy. The bitter east wind of the last few weeks had dropped, and snow-drops were lining the path in the light of the lantern.

But by daylight the first few flakes of snow were floating past the kitchen window. By mid-morning

the wind had got up and it were swirling the snow so fast, I couldn't even see the Litchfield across the street. It were no good thinking of biking anywhere in this weather; and I knowed Kate 'ud 'ave the sense not to start out from Oxford.

By three o'clock it were snowing so dense it were almost dark. I were battling up from helping Farmer Oliver with his animals, when I bumped into another snowman staggering towards me.

'My motor's in a drift along the Oxford road,' he gasped, waving vaguely over his shoulder. 'I've had to leave my wife in the snow on the side of the road; she's a cripple.'

It were obvious he were in no fit state to trudge back. I led him to the Litchfield – it were chock-a-block with folk who'd abandoned their motors – and set out to get help.

It were still snowing. Pokey Pearce were just coming out of the Alley with his lantern. I'd know his form anywhere; thin as a match with the wood scraped off, yet wiry as steel. He'd poke his nose in anywhere and flush anything out – bunkered hare, basking trout, bashful deer. 'Come on Pokey, you'd be just the chap,' I says. 'Theer's a crippled lady lying somewhere in the snow the other side of Bagnel. We can't leave her out in this; she'll be frez to d'yeth.'

He ferreted out Zicky Harris from down Alley, and fished out Eric Collett from the Bell. That made four of us, all Enstone lads; we knowed the fields around almost by instinct from early years of playing

'Fox and Hounds'. In good going, Bagnel be, at most, fifteen minutes along the road, but the road be all blocked and we was going to have to fight our way across the fields.

By now it were really dark and the snow were still swirling in the lantern light. We couldn't hurry cos we was sinking in up to our knees. It took us an hour and a half to find her.

'We gotta find a stretcher of some sort, an old gate or hurdle,' I decided. Zicky stayed put with the patient and kept hollering to each of us in turn to give us a bearing as we trampled on the tops of hedges and plunged into drifts. Pokey unearthed a hurdle and it were no picnic striving back with our burden, trying to follow remembered walls and boundaries, and getting lost over and over again in the driving snow. But us got over it. We was lucky to be in a bunch; one alone 'ud never 'ave survived. It were nigh on ten o'clock when we handed our patient safely over to Mary and Mrs Peachy at the Litchfield.

Up till then it had been a good winter, bitterly cold but open, but that week we copped the lot. Telegraph wires came down; the post couldn't get through; we was completely cut off from the outside world for over a week. There were no council snow-machines, no salting and no gritting lorries in those days. It were all shovel work.

You soon learned to shovel at a steady pace and throw with the wind. As fast as we cleared one lot, another lot flopped from the sky. After about a week, it eased up enough for us to meet up with the Spelsbury shovellers, to open the track through to Charlbury, and to clear another narrow track through Bagnel. Luckily all they motors be stuck in one direction, coming from Oxford, so the horse-mail could at last get past.

I were looking out for a fresh letter from Kate, fixing another date to get the ring. Time were pressing on. In two weeks I'd be starting my new job as head carter for Mr Hunt. Fred Ivings 'ud be moving out of the cottage, and I'd be moving in with barely a week to get it all smart and shipshape for my Kate, before our great day. I hoped our wedding flowers be still surviving, and Mr and Mrs Carey hadn't copped the same severe weather in the Vale as we had suffered in our more open Enstone.

'Present for ye!' Our Jim chucked a small postal package to me at the kitchen table. Kate's writing be that blotched from being out in the Arctic, I could barely recognise it. They was all teasing me, hankering around to see what she'd sent. Part in fun, I escaped up to my bed to be with her close in private.

'My dear Montague,
It has taken me three terrible days to pluck up the courage to write…'

'Montague'? At first glance I couldn't take it in. Then I realised the letter warn't from Kate; it were from her Mam. Her writing were very like my Kate's. I read

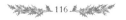

that cruel letter over and over. I couldn't believe it were anything to do with me. Gradually the icy facts, one by one, pierced home.

My Kate had set out – like all they motorists caught at Bagnel – before the snow had reached Oxford. At Kingham Junction where she had to change on to the single line to Chipping Norton, it had been blowing a blizzard for some time. The single line train had been held up by a drift the other side of Hook Norton viaduct. The next train back to Oxford didn't come for two hours. Kate must have been sickening for flu. By the time she'd spent two hours by a blazing fire in the waiting room, had a slow cold journey back to Oxford, and trudged through that freezing blizzard from the station all the way back to the infirmary, she were almost delirious. Pneumonia had set in. Because of the weather, the infirmary couldn't get in touch with her parents. Later, her parents couldn't get in touch with me. Kate never regained consciousness.

'It was a nightmare bringing our dear daughter home in her coffin on the train through the huge drifts last Wednesday, and burying her in the frozen ground of our little church… We all missed you very much. Father and I can't bear to look at the flowers in the glasshouse. They are still so beautiful and full of promise…'

Poor Mr and Mrs Carey. Jack Frost had pierced the loveliest bloom of all. My poor Kate had been out in that terrible blizzard all alone, *and I never knowed*.

'She thought the world of you, Mont. I know she would have wanted you to have this. It was always by her bedside.'

It were Kate's Sunday School bible. 'Presented to Kate Carey, 1913. Never absent, never late.' I opened it at her marker. She had marked our favourite portion of Psalms, the one we'd specially chosen for our wedding service: 'I will lift up mine eyes unto the hills.'

Never no more 'ud my lovely Kate lift her laughing blue eyes to the hills. Never no more 'ud her eyes answer mine with overwhelming love and understanding. Never no more 'ud I hear her beloved voice, smell her sweet hair, hold her soft body close.

I looked for the date of the letter. Already my Kate, my dear warm ever-loving Kate, had lain a week in the frozen ground of that little church in the Vale of Evesham. *And I never knowed.*

THE FATE OF LOVELL'S CHRISTMAS BRIDE

John Norton

*One of the most moving of all Christmas stories is associ-
ated with two great Oxfordshire mansions – Minster
Lovell Hall near Witney, which is now a ruin adminis-
tered by English Heritage, and Greys Court, the historic
National Trust property not far from Henley-on-Thames.*

Minster Lovell Hall, magnificently set on the banks
of the little River Windrush, was the home of the
Lovell family, and the story starts on the day one
Christmastime when one of the Lovells had married
his beautiful young bride. A wedding party was in
progress and there was much singing and dancing.

After a while the bride suggested a game of hide-
and-seek, hoping presumably that the first to find her
would be her new bridegroom. She scurried away
to the top of the house where in one of the rooms
she discovered an old oak chest. Seeing it as an ideal
hiding place, she climbed inside and lowered the
heavy lid. As it dropped into place, it shut fast on a
strong spring and was impossible to open again from
the inside.

The party guests searched high and low for her,
not only that evening, but for many days afterwards.
The massive timber from which the chest was made

would have masked any cries for help, and the poor young bride eventually died where she lay, in her oaken tomb.

It was not until many years later, when the bridegroom was an old man, that someone opened the old chest and discovered the skeleton of the unfortunate girl, still adorned in her wedding finery.

The elaborately carved chest still exists to this day, preserved at Greys Court, the fine house at Rotherfield Greys which passed to William, seventh Lord Lovell in the fifteenth century when he married Alice de Grey. It figures among the many treasures

The gaunt ruins of Minster Lovell Hall by the little River Windrush, all that remains of the great house where Lovell's bride met her untimely death

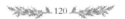

Greys Court near Henley-on-Thames counts among its treasures the 'mistletoe' chest from Minster Lovell Hall in which Lovell's bride hid and died

which visitors to Greys Court are able to see, and has become known as the 'mistletoe' chest after the tragic story surrounding it inspired the Victorian poet Thomas Haynes Bayley to write his ballad, 'The Mistletoe Bough':

> The mistletoe hung in the castle hall,
> The holly branch shone on the old oak wall;
> And the Baron's retainers were blithe and gay,
> And keeping their Christmas holiday.
> The Baron beheld with a father's pride
> His beautiful child – young Lovell's bride,
> While she with her bright eyes seem'd to be
> The star of the goodly company.

Oh! the mistletoe bough – Oh! the mistletoe bough.
'I'm weary of dancing now,' she cried;
'Here tarry a moment, I'll hide; I'll hide;
And Lovell, be sure thou'rt first to trace
The clue to my secret hiding place.'
Away she ran, and her friends began
Each tower to search and each nook to scan,
And young Lovell cried, 'Oh where dost thou hide?
I'm lonesome without thee, my own dear bride.'
Oh! the mistletoe bough – Oh! the mistletoe bough.
They sought her that night and they sought her next day,
And they sought her again, when a week passed away;
In the highest, the lowest, the loneliest spot
Young Lovell sought wildly but found her not.
And years flew by, and their grief at last
Was told as a sorrowful tale long past;
And when Lovell appeared, the children cried,
'See, the old man weeps for his fairy bride.'
Oh! the mistletoe bough – Oh! the mistletoe bough.
At length, an oak chest that long had lain hid
Was found in the castle; they raised the lid,
And a skeleton form lay mouldering there
In the bridal wreath of the lady fair.
Oh! sad was her fate! In sportive jest
She hid from her lover in the old oak chest;
It closed with a spring, and her bridal bloom
Lay withering there in a living tomb.
Oh! the mistletoe bough – Oh! the mistletoe bough.

CHRISTMAS COMMON
Colin Cox

*Oxfordshire is an area which offers rich pickings for col-
lectors of local history anecdotes, as author and journalist
Colin Cox discovered when he garnered material for a
county miscellanea in 1983. The item which follows is
deservedly included here for its festive season overtones,
although shortly after it was written, the little church
which Colin Cox mentions was declared redundant and
sold for conversion into a private residence.*

High up in the woodlands of the Chiltern Hills near
Watlington is the delightfully named hamlet of Christmas
Common, which can picturesquely justify its description
in the depths of a snowy winter, but becomes something
of an anomaly in the warm months of summer when
the sun beats down from a cloudless sky.

The origins of its name, however, are shrouded in
uncertainty, but there are several likely explanations
among others which have more than a hint of the
apocryphal about them.

One account claims that this high vantage point was
chosen by the Puritans as a site for an encampment
at Christmastime during the Civil War in the seven-
teenth century. Another harks back to the time when
much of this part of Oxfordshire was common land,
covered in dense thickets of holly. As such, it would

The aptly-named Church of the Nativity at Christmas Common, sold in recent years to become a private residence

have been a popular destination for people from the surrounding area intent upon gathering an abundance of seasonal greenery during the festive period.

Either of these explanations could well have given rise to the area becoming known as Christmas Common.

A more colourful story, no doubt invented for the benefit of childish enquirers, was that this once remote location was chosen by Santa Claus as a sort of convenient staging post during his beneficent journeyings around the county each Christmas. How his reindeer managed to negotiate all that holly when coming in to land with a fully-laden sleigh, is better left to the imagination.

One indisputable fact is that when the Victorians built the little parish church in 1889, they dedicated

it to the Holy Nativity. After all, what more apt name could there possibly be for a church serving a place called Christmas Common?

from

THIS SIDE OF THE BRIDGE
L.B. COULTHARD

Lilian Bessie Coulthard was born during the First World War at Standlake near Witney, although it is the village of Charlton-on-Otmoor between Oxford and Bicester with which she is most closely associated and where she has lived at Box Villa for many years. As a former clerk to the parish council and headmistress of the village school – which she herself attended as a child – she has always been intimately involved in village life. It is the story of this involvement on which This Side of the Bridge *is based, and her memories of village Christmases are especially evocative of the simple pleasures which were once the highlights of the festive season in rural Oxfordshire. These abridged extracts open with childhood recollections of the Christmas following the First World War, in which her father had been killed.*

When Christmas came we were very excited and hung up our pillow cases at the bottom of our beds. I was very frightened that night, as there was a fireplace near my bed and I expected a pair of legs to appear at any moment followed by a red fur-trimmed coat. But I closed my eyes and eventually fell asleep.

In the morning when I woke up, I found in the pillow case a lovely teddy bear, some books, puzzles, sweets, an orange, an apple and a few handkerchiefs.

For Christmas dinner we had roast beef with Yorkshire pudding, followed by a large Christmas pudding that Gran had made. In the evening, my mother, my auntie Elsie and my cousin Edie and I went to church for the Christmas carol service, and when we came back we were very upset to see that Gramp had taken some of the paper off the block puzzles we had been given for Christmas, to see what was underneath. Gran soothed us by telling us that she would stick them together again with paste!

On Boxing Day we were taken for a walk, and in the evening the mummers came from Weston-on-the-Green. They acted a play in the kitchen during which one of the characters, a doctor, tried to pull out a tooth. I started to cry, and I remember my mother picked me up to comfort me.

The mummers were given some home-made wine before they went on their way.

A later Christmas is marked by what was to become one of the village's traditional seasonal events, a party for the local schoolchildren.

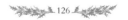

The village people held a dance once a fortnight and they decided that it would be nice to raise some money to give the schoolchildren a Christmas treat. They only paid one shilling and sixpence to go to the dance, so the amount raised towards the children's party was small. At this time there were about seventy children at the school.

So my mother agreed to go out collecting in the villages to get more money, and she went round Charlton itself, and Fencott, Murcott and Oddington.

In those days most of the children's parents worked on farms, and their weekly wages were thirty shillings. But they all gave a little towards the party, even if it was only threepence. The farmers gave about half-a-crown, as did the school managers.

Enough money was eventually raised for the party, and Mr Cartwright, the headmaster, asked my mother to order the bread, butter and paste. She also ordered the cakes and each child was allowed three, so more than fifteen dozen were bought and also some dough cake from the local baker.

The day of the party arrived. The water for the tea was boiled in an old portable copper in the school playground, and there was a marvellous spread, especially for some of the poorer children.

We all brought our own tea cups and sat at our desks to eat. The ladies came round with paste sandwiches first, and then cakes. The tea was brought round in jugs. The big boys had about ten sandwiches each, and four cakes, because the infants could not manage all theirs. Some of the boys drank ten cups of tea or more!

When the tea was finished, the children sang carols and Christmas songs, and the rector made a speech. Before we went home we were all given an apple, a bag of sweets and an orange.

As time passed, more subscriptions were collected by my mother, and in later years there was a Christmas tree with presents for all the children.

Another year and another school party – and celebrations at home at Box Villa …

Mr William Preston, the new headmaster, decided to have a Christmas party as in previous years, so my mother went out collecting round the villages again. Miss Bowler, who had the village bakehouse, was asked to be Father Christmas, as she had been the previous year. There was a big Christmas tree with presents for all the children.

In those days the presents for the top class cost about ninepence each, those for the next group sixpence, and for the infants threepence. I remember I had a pretty handkerchief and a bottle of scent. The Christmas tree was a big branch of yew given by the rector, and it was decorated with coloured candles in metal holders.

As all the parents had subscribed, Mr Preston thought that they should see something of the party, and that a play should be put on. At the end of November, his wife, who was a trained teacher, had come to the school

and read a play, *Nicholas Nickleby*. She chose the older children to act in it, and we thought it was great fun because we had only seen the infants dramatise fairy stories before. She also taught us carols to sing.

My friend Pat Crawford and I were asked to say recitations, and she said the one about Father Christmas which begins 'He comes in the night!' I recited 'When Grannie was a girl like me, her frock she never tore!'

The day of the party came and we were very excited. After the carols and play in the evening, Father Christmas gave us our presents and we were also given an orange and an apple. As we went home, we heard the church bells ringing. There was now only one day to go before Christmas.

Our house, like the others in the village, was decorated with holly, ivy and paper chains. On Christmas Eve the carol singers came round from Murcott. They came up the drive to sing, and we could still hear them singing in the distance after they had gone, because their voices carried in the frosty air.

On Christmas morning we went to church. We enjoyed the Christmas hymns which were always sung lustily, because on this particular morning there were always three or four men in the choir, besides the usual women and girls. We stayed until the end of the service and watched the adults take communion, then we went home to have our dinner. For the first time, we had a goose that year which my mother got from Tom Maycock at his farm in Wendlebury parish.

Lilian Coulthard: memories of many Christmases at Charlton-on-Otmoor

Our friend Miss Bowler came to tea as usual, and we enjoyed playing games with her as she always made us laugh. At six o'clock she went with my mother, auntie, uncle and Gramp to the carol service in church, while Edie and I stayed at home with Gran and read the books we had received for Christmas.

After church, Miss Bowler came back with the rest for supper. I remember she always brought a brick with her and asked Gran to put it in the oven. When she went she wrapped it in newspaper and took it home to warm her bed.

On Boxing Day morning we heard the church bells ringing, and Gran or my mother would get some bottles of home-made wine and mince pies ready for the ringers. They always went round the parish on Boxing Day collecting subscriptions towards the ringing, and most people gave them wine and mince pies. By the end of the day they were rather merry!

After Boxing Day we had people to tea on various days, and my friend Eric Preston came with the magic lantern he had been given for Christmas. As I had one too, we showed pictures on a tablecloth fixed to the parlour wall.

Party time again at school, dressing-up, and a fright on Boxing Day…

Another Christmas I recall was when Edie was fifteen-and-a-half, and her parents had decided that she should leave school and help with the housework. The school leaving age was then fourteen, so she had stayed a year and a half longer than she need have done.

There were more preparations than ever before for the school Christmas party. Mrs Preston had decided that all the girls in the top group should act a little

play, and she chose one called *The Gossips* which gave us all a part. The boys and the infants also did plays. That Christmas I won two prizes, one for good attendance at Sunday School and one for being top of the class.

On Boxing Day that year, Miss Bowler came to tea and afterwards she and auntie suggested that they should have a bit of fun. They planned to dress up and go round the village, auntie as a man and Miss Bowler as an old woman. I wanted to go with them, so they said that I could dress up as a boy.

Auntie put on some of Uncle Bert's old trousers, an old shirt and coat, and one of Gramp's hats. Then she made a black moustache with a cork she had burnt in a candle flame. Miss Bowler put on an old skirt of my mother's, an old blouse and hat, and draped a shawl round her shoulders.

For me, auntie found an old hat, a coat and shirt, but could not find any trousers, so she gave me a pair of new rose-pink bloomers which came down below my knees!

We went up the road giggling and laughing, but when we reached the cemetery corner we heard the most awful sounds. There were moans and clanging noises and I was very frightened. We all ran quickly past the cemetery gate, and when we looked over our shoulders we saw Gramp coming out of the cemetery. He had saucepans and lids tied round his waist with string, and he was clanging them together and moaning as he did so.

'I heard you talking about dressing-up,' he said, 'so I thought I would have some fun too.'

In spite of our fright, we had a lot of fun that Christmas.

Another Christmas never to be forgotten, when deep snow mantled the Oxfordshire countryside…

On Christmas Day the wind was blowing and howling down the chimney. I was sitting on a stool by the fire holding two balloons tied to a piece of string. Suddenly a gust of wind took both of them straight up the chimney, and where they went I shall never know.

It continued blowing, and snow started to fall. When the grown-ups came back from the carol service at church there was a carpet of about two inches of snow on the ground. It snowed all night, and as the wind blew fiercely there were drifts in many places by the morning.

Round the corner from Box Villa there were mounds of snow at least six feet high. It even covered the hedges, and the roadmen and their helpers had to dig a path through.

Still it continued snowing, and we heard that the milk lorry was stuck in a drift. In those days the lorry came daily from Aylesbury to collect the milk from the farms and take it to the Nestle's factory where it was used to make chocolate, or condensed and put into tins.

It was quite dark when Gramp heard about the milk lorry and he said he was going to have a look.

Filling his hurricane lamp with paraffin and putting on his thick overcoat, he was ready to set off. He said I could go too, so I put on my laced boots, wrapped up warm and followed in his footsteps. It made me think of the page in 'Good King Wenceslas' – in his master's steps he trod.

When we reached the lorry, men were digging it out and there were boys there too, helping them. The drifts were by then about seven feet high and Gramp said he thought we had better return home.

By now a young trainee schoolteacher, Lilian Coulthard involves herself in the celebrations for yet another Christmas, and again the weather has a seasonal edge to it…

My mother collected money as usual for the school Christmas party which was planned for 'breaking-up' day, complete with a big Christmas tree. Mrs Preston came again to produce the various plays, and I spent some of the time watching the rehearsals or went to the infants' room to look after the little ones. Helping in the school as a pupil-teacher was all part of my teacher training, and because it was the end of term I was not so busy with the homework set by the tutors in Oxford where I had to attend classes once a week.

After Christmas there were many hard frosts – the old men called them black frosts – and soon the floods and ponds and rivers were frozen over. Girls, boys, men and women were all skating on the ice, and we went to watch. The temperature in the school was very low, not reaching more than 48 degrees on some days, and there was a lot of illness in the village.

The term passed quickly and soon it was Christmas again. The headmaster at Ambrosden gave the children a party, and his wife came in from Bicester with sandwiches and cakes.

I thought it would be nice if the children could entertain their parents with a play, as they did at Charlton, so I organised one for the juniors in my class. They had not acted before, and one or two were very nervous. In fact, one of them cried in the middle which rather spoilt it!

The children enjoyed their party at Ambrosden, and I was lucky enough also to be able to go to the party back home in Charlton, as it was being held on the following day. That Christmas I was feeling very excited because I was to be a bridesmaid for the first time, to one of my cousins at Standlake. My mother made the dress. It was a deep cream, with blue and orange flowers, and a frill round the bottom.

This final extract from Lilian Coulthard's recollections finds her having moved from Ambrosden to a new school at Wootton, near Woodstock. She has bought a car, and it's Christmas again…

Autumn passed quickly, and soon preparations for Christmas were once more being made.

On my way home from school one day, I came through the village of Oddington to pick up my

mother in the car and take her home. She had been out on her rounds again, collecting for the Christmas party.

She told me that she had heard the news that Edward VIII was abdicating in favour of his brother Albert, Duke of York, because the Prime Minister and the Archbishop of Canterbury would not give their consent for him to marry the American lady Mrs Wallis Simpson, as she was a divorcee.

That night we listened to his farewell speech on the radio, when he said he could not carry on being king without the help of the woman he loved, and that he was giving up the throne to his brother. That Christmas the village children sang their own version of a popular carol: 'Hark the herald angels sing, Mrs Simpson stole our king'!

CHRISTMAS AT BLENHEIM
His Grace The Duke Of Marlborough

Blenheim Palace near Woodstock, Sir John Vanbrugh's Classical masterpiece, is one of the best-known stately mansions in England. Home of the eleventh Duke of Marlborough and birthplace of Sir Winston Churchill, it welcomes tens of thousands of visitors every year. Each Christmas, during a respite from its role as a major tourist attraction, Blenheim comes into its own as a family home, witnessing the traditional celebrations which are still an essential ingredient of the festive season. The Duke of Marlborough describes them here.

The Christmas celebrations at Blenheim start with the estate children's party which is usually held on 23 December. There is an entertainer for the little ones, and after tea Father Christmas arrives with his presents. The party ends with the traditional carol singing.

Christmas at Blenheim has always been a family affair following great traditions, when young and old gather to celebrate together the birth of Christ. The private chapel is used on Christmas Eve for a short communion service.

Christmas Day itself is filled with the opening of stockings, going to the Christmas service at Woodstock, and over-indulging in turkey and mince

Historic Blenheim Palace at Woodstock, a fine setting for a family Christmas

pies and other delights. There is also the opening of the presents put out under the Christmas tree, which traditionally stands in the bow window of the dining room, with all its lights reflected in the mirrors between the windows. The Queen's speech on television is watched by everyone.

Before 1939, the family lived in the entire house, and the Saloon was the main dining room. Today it is used once a year by the family on Christmas night. Although the Palace is hardly ever silent, and other parties are held in the State Apartments and Long Library, it is on Christmas night that Blenheim really seems to come alive. The Pollard oak dining table is extended to its full length to seat 40 members of the family and friends, and it is laid with the Marlborough silver. Two huge open fires sparkle, and there are flowers, candelabra, Christmas crackers and other decorations to make the occasion a truly spectacular sight.

NATIVITY
JOHN DONNE

Poet, preacher and Dean of St Paul's, John Donne (1573–1631) had the distinction of being admitted to Hart Hall, Oxford, at the remarkably young age of twelve, although it was at Cambridge that he eventually graduated. His considerable literary output embraced a wide range of poetry and prose, and included satyrical works, sermons, letters and a collection of divine poems recounting the story of Christ, from which Nativity *is taken.*

Immensity cloister'd in thy dear womb,
Now leaves His well-belov'd imprisonment,
There he hath made Himself to His intent
Weak enough, now into our world to come;
But Oh, for thee, for Him, hath th' Inn no room?
Yet lay Him in this stall, and from the Orient,
Stars, and wise men will travel to prevent
Th' effect of Herod's jealous general doom.

See'st thou, my Soul, with thy faith's eyes, how He
Which fills all place, yet none holds Him, doth lie?
Was not His pity towards thee wondrous high,
That would have need to be pitied by thee?
Kiss Him, and with Him into Egypt go,
With His kind mother, who partakes thy woe.

TWELFTH CAKE AND SNAP-DRAGON
J. A. R. PIMLOTT

In an earlier extract from The Englishman's Christmas
*John Pimlott described how Oxford played a significant
part in the resurrection of the old custom of carol singing
in the last century. In this second selection from his work,
he writes of seasonal traditions which were less fortunate
at the hands of the Victorians, and today rarely, if ever,
contribute to our Christmastide celebrations.*

Of the casualties which occurred in the nineteenth
century none would have astonished previous generations more than the virtual disappearance of the
Twelfth-tide celebrations. Though already attenu-
ated, Twelfth Night in the thirties and forties still
ranked with Christmas Day as one of the greatest
of the twelve. It was the climax of the festive season,
marked by gay parties, the Twelfth cake and the time-

honoured ritual: the King and Queen and their Court were now almost always chosen by drawing the pictorial Twelfth 'characters' which the inventive made for themselves and most people bought from the stationer or the confectioner.

In the sixties the custom was noted as dying out, although Twelfth parties and 'characters' continue to be mentioned throughout the century – they were referred to in *Punch* in the nineties – but in 1911 so little was left of them that a correspondent could write in *The Times* that only the cake remained of the Twelfth-tide celebrations, except in remote parts where folk customs like wassailing the apple trees were kept up.

The Twelfth cake 'culminating in a Harlequin' which Dickens described in *Edwin Drood* in the seventies exemplifies the transition. Its days of glory over, it was 'poor' and 'little' and it was raffled at a pastry-cook's on Christmas Eve.

The raffling of Twelfth cakes was not new – it happened at Oxford in the fifties – but it was surely a sign of degeneration, and the fact that the raffling took place on Christmas Eve shows that the custom had shifted from Twelfth Night.

It also gives a clue to the future of the Twelfth cake. Twelfth-tide shrivelled away, but its customs were not wholly lost to the English Christmas. It is likely that the coins and trinkets which are still – despite the use of cupro-nickel in the 'silver' coinage since the early 1920s – sometimes boiled in the Christmas

pudding, are descended from the bean and the pea of the Twelfth cake: the bean and pea were sometimes replaced by silver replicas.

And what is the Christmas cake but the Twelfth cake, attracted as at Cloisterham in *Edwin Drood* to Christmas Day itself? It was never mentioned until the Twelfth cake was going out, and coincidence could not explain the appearance of a second plum cake, iced and decorated, and though diminished in splendour, identical except in name with its famous predecessor.

It is harder to account for the disappearance of another group of customs which had long been inseparable from the English Christmas and continued to flourish well into the middle of the century.

In one form or another hot and spiced drinks were regarded as essential to Christmas at all social levels. The upper classes drank their 'punch', and there were many recipes each cherished by those who were accustomed to use it. 'Poor man's punch' was made with ale instead of rum or brandy. The hot and spiced elderberry wine of many country districts was another variation, and all were variations on the traditional wassail drink. 'Welcome Christmas', the Royalist pamphleteer had said in 1652, ''tis our desire to give thee more spiced ale'.

And what was the reason for the disappearance of 'snap-dragon'? Hervey was 'not a little anxious' about its future in 1836, but most Victorian writers took it completely for granted. Chambers said that it was generally played on Christmas Eve. Brandy was poured over raisins and lit. The lights were put out, and in the eerie darkness each person in turn snatched a raisin from the flames. It was 'somewhat of an arduous feast, requiring both courage and rapidity of action; a considerable amount of laughter and merriment is evoked at the expense of the unsuccessful competitors'.

For those who could not afford snap-dragon, there was the alternative of 'flap-dragon' which was still kept up by the poorer people in some areas. It was at least as old as Shakespeare: 'and drinks off candled ends for flap-dragons', said Falstaff in *Henry IV Part II*. In this pastime, the object was to drain a can of ale or cider, in the mouth of which there was a lighted candle.

Clearly, as Mrs Ewing said in 1872, snap-dragon had 'mysterious and pungent pleasures' to offer, and the scene around the bowl comes to vivid life in 'The Song of Snap-Dragon' which was quoted by Chambers and other writers, and was supposedly chanted during the proceedings:

Here he comes with flaming bowl,
Don't he mean to take his toll,
 Snip! Snap! Dragon!
Take care you don't take too much,
Be not greedy in your clutch,
 Snip! Snap! Dragon!
With his blue and leaping tongue

Many of you will be stung.
    Snip! Snap! Dragon!
For he snaps at all that comes
Snatching at his feast of plums,
    Snip! Snap! Dragon!
But old Christmas makes his court,
Though he looks so fee! fa! fum!
    Snip! Snap! Dragon!
Don't 'ee fear him, be but bold,
Out he goes, his flames are cold,
    Snip! Snap! Dragon!

As one writer pointed out, ladies had to be careful not to catch their dresses on fire (flap-dragon was more dangerous to beards and moustaches), but concern with safety can scarcely explain the more or less sudden passing of a traditional party amusement which to its other attractions added an element of the ghostly so much in keeping with the season, and like cake, mince pie and pudding, embodied the 'plums' so long associated with it. Is it fanciful to suggest that traces of 'snap-dragon' remain in the custom of burning brandy over the Christmas pudding?

from

THE FATHER CHRISTMAS LETTERS

J. R. R. TOLKIEN

Tolkien was a prolific writer for children, best known for his classic works The Lord of the Rings *and* The Hobbit. *For many years the family home was in Oxford, and Tolkien's associations with the city were numerous. He graduated at the university and later held important posts there including Rawlinson and Bosworth Professor of Anglo-Saxon, and Merton Professor of English Language and Literature. He was a Fellow of Merton College, and in 1972 – a year before he died at the age of 81 – the university conferred on him an Honorary Doctorate of Letters. When his children were young, he invented a fantasy world for their benefit, based on the North Pole home of Father Christmas who, each year at Christmastime, sent the children elaborately illustrated letters. These were eventually published as a collection, edited by Tolkien's daughter-in-law Baillie, and the example reproduced after the following introduction was dated Christmas 1939, the last to be written.*

The annual letters which Tolkien's children received from Father Christmas described in words and pictures his house and his friends, and the extraordinary variety of events which took place at the North Pole.

The first of the letters arrived in 1920 when John, the eldest, was three years old, and for some twenty years, through the childhoods of the three other children, Michael, Christopher and Priscilla, they continued to arrive each Christmas.

Sometimes the envelopes, suitably dusted with snow and bearing North Pole postage stamps, were discovered in the house on the morning after Father Christmas's annual visit; at other times the postman delivered them. Letters in reply which the children wrote themselves, mysteriously vanished from the fireplace when no-one was about.

As time went on, Father Christmas's household became larger. At first, little was written about anyone else except Polar Bear, but later there was mention of Snow-elves, Red Gnomes, Snowmen, Cave-bears, and the Polar Bear's nephews, Paksu and Valkotukka. But the Polar Bear himself remained Father Christmas's chief assistant and the main cause of the disasters which were blamed for muddles and deficiencies in the Christmas stockings.

The children received this last Christmas letter from the North Pole in 1939, shortly after the outbreak of the Second World War:

> I am so glad you did not forget to write to me again this year. The number of children who keep up with me seems to be getting smaller. I expect it is because of this horrible war, and that when it is over things will improve

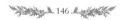

Father Christmas arrives over Oxford, his sleigh pulled by seven pairs of reindeer, led by one white pair. This is one of Tolkien's original and highly imaginative drawings which he used to illustrate the letters from Father Christmas to his children

again, and I shall be as busy as ever. But at present so terribly many people have lost their homes, or have left them; half the world seems in the wrong place! And even up here we have been having troubles. I don't mean only with my stores; of course they are getting low. They were already low last year, and I have not been able to fill them up, so that I have to send what I can, instead of what is asked for. But worse than that has happened.

I expect you remember that some years ago we had trouble with the Goblins, and we thought we had settled it. Well it broke out again this autumn, worse than it has been for centuries. We have had several battles, and for a while my house was besieged. In November it began to look likely that it would be captured, and all my goods, and that Christmas stockings would remain empty all over the world. Would not that have been a calamity?

It has not happened – and that is largely due to the efforts of Polar Bear – but it was not until the beginning of this month that I was able to send out any messengers! I expect the Goblins thought that with so much war going on, this was a fine chance to recapture the North. They must have been preparing for some years; and they made a huge new tunnel which had an outlet many miles away. It was in early October that they suddenly came out in thousands. Polar Bear says that there were at least a million, but that is his favourite big number. Anyway he was still fast asleep at the time, and I was rather drowsy myself.

The weather was rather warm for the time of the year, and Christmas seemed far away. There were only one or two Elves about the place; and of course Paksu and Valkotukka (also fast asleep). Luckily Goblins cannot help yelling and beating on drums when they mean to fight; so we all woke up in time, and got the gates and doors barred and the windows shuttered. Polar Bear got on the roof and fired rockets into the Goblin hosts as they poured up the long reindeer-drive; but that did not stop them for long.

We were soon surrounded. I have not time to tell you all the story. I had to blow three blasts on the great Horn (Windbeam). It hangs over the fireplace in the hall, and if I have not told you about it before, it is because I have not had to blow it for over four hundred years. Its sound carries as far as the North Wind blows. All the same, it was three whole days before help came: Snow-boys, Polar Bears, and hundreds and hundreds of Elves. They came up behind the Goblins; and Polar Bear (really awake this time) rushed out with a blazing branch off the fire in each paw. He must have killed dozens of Goblins (he says a million).

But there was a big battle down in the plain near the North Pole in November, in which the Goblins brought hundreds of new companies out of their tunnels. We were driven back to the Cliff, and it was not until Polar Bear and a party of his younger relatives crept out by night, and blew up the entrance to the new tunnels with nearly 100 lbs of gunpowder, that we got the better of them – for the present. But bang went all the stuff for making fireworks and crackers (the cracking part) for some years. The North Pole cracked and fell over (for the second time) and we have not yet had time to mend it. Polar Bear is rather a hero (I hope he does not think so himself). But of course he is a very *magical* animal really, and Goblins can't do much to him when he is awake and angry. I have seen their arrows bouncing off him and breaking.

Well that will give you some idea of events, and you will understand why I have not had time to draw a picture this year – rather a pity, because there have been such exciting things to draw – and why I have not been able to collect the usual things for you, or even the very few that you asked for.

I suppose after this year you will not be hanging your stockings any more. I shall have to say goodbye, more or less: I mean, I shall not forget you. We always keep the names of our old friends, and their letters; and later on we hope to come back when they are grown up and have houses of their own and children.

FATHER CHRISTMAS

CHRISTMAS AT BANBURY
∫NON

The First World War had been raging for more than a
year, although it was all a long way from Banbury and
did not impinge too seriously on the town's celebration of
Christmas. But as one newspaper columnist reported on
22 December 1915, the local people had not forgotten 'the
gallant men on active service' during that festive season, even
if the unfortunate inmates of the workhouse were denied
their customary allocation of beer.

The butchers and poultry-dealers have had a busy
time in preparation for the Christmas festival. All
the prize stock at the Fat Stock Show was purchased
locally, and there were some fine displays during the
weekend. Trade locally is fairly brisk and there is little
distress in the town, as sometimes happens at this
time. The townspeople have responded liberally to
the appeals for Christmas presents for our soldiers and
sailors, and large consignments have been sent to our
gallant men on active service.

There will be the usual Christmas fare at the
workhouse, although the proceedings at the Board
of Guardians on Thursday were somewhat amusing. For years there has been an annual fight as to
whether the inmates should have beer on Christmas
Day, and last year, for the first time in the history of

A reminder of a wintry Christmas season in the Banbury area around the time of the First World War. This photograph was taken in the village of Adderbury

the Union, beer was not allowed by the Board, but it was given privately.

This year, however, the House Committee recommended that no beer be provided by the Board or given by any private individuals, and the report was adopted on a misunderstanding. There had been a debate on another question, the report was put and carried before the beer party had time to see their mistake, and the Chairman ruled all further discussion out of order. On Thursday Mr Crawford Wood was unsuccessful in getting the standing orders suspended, so could not get in a motion that beer be allowed. He then proposed that the inmates have the regulation quantity of rum allowed by the Local Government Board, and this was lost by only two votes.

The Banbury workhouse was obviously not the place to be during that particular Christmas period – despite the laudable efforts of Mr Crawford Wood.

from

JOG-TROT DAYS
WILFRED BURSON

In 1922 Wilfred Burson was still at school in Chipping Norton. One day his teacher said to the class: 'Write down 22.2.22, for that is today's date, and take notice that it's all twos. In fifty-five years' time when I am dead and gone, many of you will be able to write a date which is all sevens – 7.7.77. I want you to try to imagine what life will be like then.' Wilfred Burson lived to find out for himself, and the changes proved to be so great that he determined to set down a record of his childhood in the 1920s before the memories were lost for ever. He did this in Jog-Trot Days, *published in 1980, and it is a graphic account of how day-to-day life was lived in those far-off times in and around his beloved Chipping Norton – or 'Chippy' as most people knew it. He called the chapter reproduced here 'Winter's Tale'.*

In 1922 we were almost at the end of a period of hot summers and very hard winters, with rivers and lakes frozen solid for months. The seasons were changing, though in the 1920s we still had lots of hot weather in summer and plenty of snow and ice in winter. There were times when the ground was covered with snow for several weeks; each evening the sun set like a ball of fire and there was a heavy frost.

Sometimes villages and towns were cut off by snowdrifts, and this really did mean cut off. No vehicles could get in or out, and folk just had to stay put. Wind blew the snow across hills and fields, and it built up on roads between hedges, causing drifts five or six feet deep.

There were no mechanical snow ploughs, only horse-drawn ones, and these were of little use. Teams of men had to dig a way through with shovels, and when darkness fell they left off until next morning, often leaving a wall of snow higher than themselves.

In most villages water had to be carried in buckets from communal taps, each of which served several cottages, and when the frost was severe the problem was to prevent the supply freezing up. Sacking was tied round the taps and pipes, and rags soaked in paraffin were burned underneath them. But even then there were times when no water came through and folk had to melt the snow.

Lakes were solid enough for skating, and we boys learned to skate the hard way – by falling down until we got the knack of remaining on our feet!

Many of the big houses had a lake in the grounds, and when it was frozen, folk were allowed to go and

'Teams of men had to dig a way through with shovels…'

skate. Often, the people from the house joined in, and on several occasions we skated with lords and ladies by the light of the moon until late in the evening.

Young people in the country enjoyed sledging, and every family kept a sledge which was brought out of the wood shed at the beginning of winter and the runners polished with care. There were plenty of hills to sledge down, and hours of happiness were spent in toiling uphill with the sledge, then hurtling down at breakneck speed.

Old people found the winters particularly trying, and many who lived with their married children stayed indoors from the beginning of winter until the following spring. They sat close to the fire to keep as warm as they could in the draughty cottages.

'Every family kept a sledge, which was brought out of the wood shed at the beginning of winter…'

Apart from the fire in the living room, there was no other heating except perhaps an oil heater which, in those days before 'pink' paraffin, was very liable to smoke. Folk used to say: 'It were that cold in our bedroom last night, the chamber pot froze solid.'

In the small towns things were not quite so bad, and horse-drawn snow ploughs were brought into action as soon as the snow began to get deep. At least folk were able to get about and attend to their business and shopping, though at times it was difficult.

The milkman, who brought fresh milk from Rollright, a village three or four miles from Chippy, often found he had to get through a foot of snow, and this meant harnessing sometimes three horses to his milk float instead of the usual single one. In the float were several churns of milk 'straight from the cows', which was delivered to the houses in open milk buckets and ladled into people's jugs with pint or half-pint measures. There was very little regard for hygiene in those days!

I remember one winter's morning in our district, in about 1927, the like of which had never been experienced even by the oldest folk. It had been fine for over a week, but the day before it had rained heavily, leaving water everywhere. During the night there was a drastic change in the weather, and a very hard frost set in which meant that by morning everything outside was covered with ice. Roofs and walls of houses, doorsteps and pathways, roads and even the grass verges were iced over, and folk stepping out of their houses in the early morning darkness immediately crashed to the ground.

Horses could not stand, and only by wrapping sacking round their boots could people move at all. Some put on skates and managed to get to work that way, but others just stayed indoors.

Long icicles hung everywhere and the countryside looked as it had never looked within living memory. During the afternoon, the weather changed again, the ice quickly melted and things got back to normal, but many people were nursing injuries caused by falling.

Winter epidemics struck from time to time, and one season there was a particularly bad 'flu epidemic which caused the death of many in our district. In the country, people just went to bed and kept as warm

'The milkman who brought fresh milk from Rollright, often found he had to get through a foot of snow…'

as they could; there were no injections or tablets, not even aspirins in those days. When someone in a village was off work through illness, it was said: 'Ee be bad abed'.

In Chippy three well-known shopkeepers died within a matter of weeks, along with many other people. The grave digger at the cemetery had a tough time getting the graves ready, and afterwards he said: 'That was the wust time I remembers. I 'ad to work seven days a wick, an' that be summat I never done afore.'

There was a custom that if someone was very ill in a bedroom overlooking a road or street, straw was placed on the road in front of the house to reduce the noise from horses' hooves and the wheels of passing vehicles. Also by custom, when a death took place in a house, all the window blinds were drawn until after the funeral, and on the day of the funeral blinds were drawn at nearby houses too. As the funeral procession passed along the street, people and vehicles stopped, and as the coffin passed by, men stood and removed their hats.

Christmas was, of course, the happiest time of the year, and families did their best to get together. Often folk made difficult journeys through snow to be at home on Christmas Day, and it was a time of happiness and rejoicing.

During the days before Christmas, children made coloured paper chains and gathered holly from the hedges. Housewives prepared food in readiness, and excitement began to build up, but it was not until Christmas Eve that the decorations were put up. Then the boys and girls went off to bed early, after hanging up their stockings, so as to be awake early on Christmas morning.

When they awoke, they found in their stockings an apple, an orange and sweets, and perhaps a few small toys, plus dolls for the girls. There were no elaborate presents such as children get these days. With wages of two or three pounds a week, and no such thing as a family allowance, parents could not afford more, but children were much more appreciative and happy with what they got.

New Street, Chipping Norton, after a heavy fall of snow – a scene which
Wilfred Burson still recalls vividly from his childhood

Later came the postman, bringing Christmas cards
and perhaps parcels from distant relatives. In those days
there was a morning delivery on Christmas Day, and
everyone looked forward to greeting the postman.

Dinner was a big meal, with Christmas pudding
and mince pies, and crackers with paper hats in them,
and there were games right through the afternoon
until tea time. Then there was Christmas cake with
icing and a Father Christmas on it. It was the children's day, and they were allowed to stay up very late
and join in the evening's fun.

On Boxing Day morning there was always a meet
of one of the hunts not very far away, and people
walked or cycled to see it. The Boxing Day meet
was a big social occasion; the wealthy hunt members
were in great form and high spirits following all the

feasting, drinking and Christmas celebrations of the day before. When the hunt moved off from the meet, most of those who had gone to watch went home, but the regular followers on foot or bicycle kept up with them as best they could for the rest of the day.

There were many poor and sick people who couldn't enjoy Christmas, and so every year the choir from the Baptist chapel went carol singing each evening for over a week before Christmas, and with the money collected they made up parcels of groceries and presented them to such people. It was quite a tradition in Chippy, and people gave generously. In that way, many of the needy were given a little happiness at Christmastime.

It was back to work on the day after Boxing Day, unless that day happened to be a Sunday, and so Christmas was soon over for another year. All that remained was to welcome the New Year. There was always a New Year's Eve dance at the Town Hall, and a watch night service for chapel people. The bells of the parish church rang out at midnight.

With the coming of the New Year, days began to lengthen, and folk looked for the first signs that winter was nearly over – snowdrops and crocuses, and lambs in the fields. Soon the frost and snow would be gone, and then, in March, daffodils would begin to bloom and before long it would be spring again.

WELL, SO THAT IS THAT

W.H. Auden

*Although Wystan Hugh Auden (1907–73) was born
and educated in England, he took American citizenship
in 1939. While studying at Christ Church, Oxford, he
edited* Oxford Poetry, *and was Professor of Poetry at
the university from 1956 to 1961. He wrote* Well, So
That is That *in 1944, an incisive and thought-provoking
commentary on post-Christmas attitudes.*

Well, so that is that. Now we must dismantle the tree,
Putting the decorations back into their cardboard boxes
  –
Some have got broken – and carrying them up into the
  attic.
The holly and the mistletoe must be taken down and
  burnt,
And the children got ready for school. These are enough
Left overs to do, warmed-up, for the rest of the week –
Not that we have much appetite, having drunk such a
  lot,
Stayed up so late, attempted – quite unsuccessfully –
To love all our relatives, and in general
Grossly overestimated our powers. Once again
As in previous years we have seen the actual Vision and
  failed
To do more than entertain it as an agreeable

Possibility. Once again we have sent Him away,

Begging though to remain His obedient servant,

The promising child who cannot keep His word for
   long.

The Christmas Feast is already a fading memory,

And already the mind begins to be vaguely aware

Of an unpleasant whiff of apprehension at the thought

Of Lent and Good Friday which cannot, after all, now

Be very far off. But, for the time being, here we all are,

Back in the moderate Aristotelian city

Of darning and the Eight-Fifteen, where Euclid's
   geometry

And Newton's mechanics would account for our experience,

And the kitchen table exists because I scrub it.

It seems to have shrunk during the holidays. The streets

Are much narrower than we remembered; we had forgotten

The office was as depressing as this. To those who have
   seen

The Child, however dimly, however incredulously,

The Time Being is, in a sense, the most trying time of
   all.

For the innocent children who whispered so excitedly

Outside the locked door where they knew the presents
   to be,

Grew up when it opened. Now, recollecting the
   moment

We can repress the joy, but the guilt remains conscious;

Remembering the stable where for once in our lives

162

Everything became a You and nothing was an It.
And craving the sensation but ignoring the cause,
We look round for something, no matter what, to inhibit
Our self-reflection, and the obvious thing for that purpose
Would be some great suffering. So, once we have met the Son,
We are tempted ever after to pray to the Father:
'Lead us not into temptation and evil for our sake'.
They will come all right, don't worry; probably in a form
That we do not expect, and certainly with a force
More dreadful than we can imagine. In the meantime
There are bills to be paid, machines to keep in repair,
Irregular verbs to learn, the Time Being to redeem
From insignificance. The happy morning is over,
The night of agony still to come; the time is noon:
When the Spirit must practise his scales of rejoicing
Without even a hostile audience, and the Soul endure
A silence that is neither for nor against her faith
That God's Will will be done, that, in spite of her prayers,
God will cheat no one, not even the world of its triumph.

THE BOXING DAY WREN HUNT
CHARLES CUNNINGHAM

*There was a time when village folk in many parts of
the country participated in one of the strangest of all
Christmas traditions. It involved the killing of the most
endearing of our native birds, the tiny wren, and it gained
a particularly ardent following in Oxfordshire. This
description of it from the pen of country writer Charles
Cunningham, puts the curious custom into perspective.*

The Feast of Stephen, on which day, as the carol
says, good King Wenceslas looked out, is of course
now more widely known as Boxing Day. For
most people it is a time to recover from the over-
indulgence of the previous day, either by closeting
themselves in their homes in front of the television,
or, for the more energetic, taking a brisk walk in the
country, perhaps to take part in one of the traditional
Boxing Day meets.

But at one time, Boxing Day was the occasion for
one of the most unusual of all the old Christmastide
customs, which attracted large numbers of both participants and onlookers. This was the wren hunt, a
seemingly barbaric tradition which today would pro-
voke an angry public outcry if it were still practised.

Its origins are obscure, but there are records link-
ing it with the Druids who had devised some method

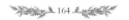

of prophesying the future by capturing a wren and then studying the individual notes of its song. Another theory suggests that St Stephen – the first Christian martyr – was betrayed by the singing of the wren while he was attempting to escape from his captors, and the poor bird was then punished by death. This version sounds no less apocryphal than the Druid story.

Whatever the explanation, the wren hunt once flourished over much of the country, and nowhere with more enthusiasm than in Oxfordshire, where the villagers looked forward to it each year with relish. Its wide popularity is all the more difficult to comprehend when one considers that at any other time of the year, the wren, like the robin, was regarded almost as a sacred bird which should never be harmed. In

The endearing wren, once mercilessly hunted at Christmastime as part of an ancient custom

Nowadays, a meet of the local hunt is one of the more popular seasonal traditions on St Stephen's Day, or Boxing Day – a fact for which the wren population is, no doubt, eternally grateful. This 1962 photograph shows the Heythrop Hunt at Chipping Norton

fact, there was a country rhyme which made this abundantly clear:

> The robin and the redbreast,
> The robin and the wren,
> If ye take out of the nest,
> Ye'll never thrive again.

Another old saying decreed:

> Kill a robin or a wren,
> Never prosper, boy or man.

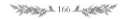

Yet once a year, convention was turned on its head, and this unfortunate creature was hunted and killed. The tiny corpse was fixed to the end of a long stake decorated with holly and ivy, and paraded through the villages to the accompaniment of much merriment and drum-beating and the singing of the traditional wren hunt song:

> The wren, the wren, the king of all birds,
> On St Stephen's Day was caught in the furze.
> Although he is little, his family is great,
> I pray you, good dame, do give us a treat.

Some villagers exchanged the decorated stake for a hooped garland, with the dead bird as a centrepiece, while others of a more superstitious nature would pluck the wren's feathers and sell them to help ward off evil spirits until the next St Stephen's Day. In any event, there was always keen competition among men and boys to be the first to kill a wren, as this gave the killer special status and guaranteed him good luck for a whole year.

But whatever form the curious custom took, the principal motive was usually the collecting of money, and while one group of merrymakers paraded the dead wren through the streets and sang the traditional song, others would call at the houses hoping for a suitably generous donation.

In more enlightened areas – which, according to the records, did not include Oxfordshire – the little wren was not killed, but placed in a cage or 'wren house', and then released again after the parade was over. But even in these circumstances, the poor creature often died anyway – presumably of fright.

Mercifully, this strange custom died out long ago, and nowadays the wrens of Oxfordshire, as elsewhere, have no need to fear Boxing Day or any other time for that matter, except of course when the winter weather is severe. On these occasions, the wren's mortality rate is high – but the blame then falls on Nature rather than on a cruel Christmastide custom of Man.

from

ELIZA OF OTMOOR
Phyllis Surman

Phyllis Surman wrote Eliza of Otmoor *in 1975, a moving biography of her grandmother Eliza Haynes, who was born in the Otmoor village of Noke near Oxford in 1850. Described as a 'courageous and independent lady', Eliza had seven children in nine years – Esther, Ada, Eva, George, Alma, Leah and May – and after the sudden death of her husband, she had the formidable task of bringing up her large family single-handed on a pittance of an income. By 1900 she was on the domestic staff of Oriel College, Oxford, thanks to the benevolence of a*

Fellow of the College and Doctor of Divinity, Dr L.R. Phelps. The family – except for Esther who was away 'in service' – lived in a small house in the city, and Christmas that year, after so much deprivation, was to prove a happy time for them all.

There was a college party for the servants' children, and all the girls went, feeling very smart, with new pinafores, trimmed with lace. There was a huge Christmas tree from which they received a present. May had a tin train with three carriages, which seemed an odd gift for a little girl, but with which she played for some time before handing it on to George. When it came to Alma's turn, Father Christmas said: 'For Alma Haynes, the game of Halma', which made them all laugh.

Afterwards there was tea, refreshments and 'living pictures', and as they walked home together in the cold darkness of a December night, they all agreed it had been a wonderful party.

The following day, Eliza was sent for by Dr Phelps, who received her, as always, with great courtesy. He explained that at Christmas it was his custom to make gifts of poultry to his staff, and gave her the name of a poulterer in the market where she might go and choose her Christmas dinner.

Eliza thanked him warmly for this gesture, and on her way home called at the market and chose a turkey which cost ten shillings. When this creature was displayed before the assembled family, it was greeted with oohs and aahs of admiration, prodded and stroked, then hung on a hook in the larder.

Christmas Day itself started with the ceremonial emptying of stockings, usually containing dates wrapped in coloured paper, an orange, apple and some nuts. The turkey came up to all expectations, a golden, sizzling creature now, on a big willow-patterned dish, after which the blinds were drawn and Eliza brought in a holly-topped, sugar-sprinkled pudding, which had been set alight with brandy, and this was a further delight. Usually, there was a bottle of wine, or lemonade, according to taste, and the whole family stood for what was known to them as the family 'toast'.

Here's to them that we love,
And to them that love us.
Here's to all them that love them,
That love them that love us.

In the evening there were games, the favourite of which was 'Snap-Dragon'. Raisins spread on a large flat dish were fired with brandy, so that one was obliged to grab quickly from the flames as many raisins as possible. These were afterwards counted and the possessor of the most raisins awarded a small prize.

Later, when the younger children were in bed, Eliza sat chatting to her older children in the glow of the dying fire. She was ever grateful for the companionship of her family, and they, ever appreciative of the efforts of this tiny matriarch.

Eliza Haynes (centre) surrounded by her seven children. Back row, left to right: Esther, Eva and Ada. Middle Row: George and Alma. Front row: May and Leah

PREPARATIONS
Anon

*These meaningful verses on the theme of preparing for
the religious significance of Christmas were penned by
an anonymous seventeenth-century poet whose original
manuscript is preserved at Christ Church, Oxford.*

Yet if His Majesty, our sovran lord,
Should of his own accord
Friendly himself invite,
And say 'I'll be your guest tomorrow night',
How should we stir ourselves, call and command
All hands to work. 'Let no man idle stand!

'Set me fine Spanish tables in the hall;
See they be fitted all;
Let there be room to eat
And order taken that there want no meat.
See every sconce and candlestick made bright,
That without tapers they may give a light.

'Look to the presence: are the carpets spread,
The dazie o'er the head,
The cushions in the chairs,
And all the candles lighted on the stairs?
Perfume the chambers, and in any case
Let each man give attendance in his place.'

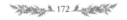

Thus, if a king were coming, would we do;
And 'twere good reason too;
For 'tis a duteous thing
To show all honour to an earthly king,
And after all our travail and our cost,
So he be pleased, to think no labour lost.

But at the coming of the King of Heaven
All's set at six and seven;
We wallow in our sin,
Christ cannot find a chamber in the inn.
We entertain Him always like a stranger,
And, as at first, still lodge Him in the manger.

from

LINGER AWHILE
JACK CALLOW

Jack Callow's Linger Awhile *is a nostalgic collection of nearly thirty stories of life in the 1920s in his home village of Souldern between Bicester and Banbury. His memories of Christmas, abridged here from chapters entitled 'Our Christmas' and 'Christmas Party', provide a glimpse of the simple childhood pleasures which characterised the festive season in those far-off days, long before television and blatant commercialisation brought their irrevocable influences to bear, and changed attitudes for ever.*

Three to four weeks before Christmas, Mother would have the ingredients all ready for the Christmas puddings and mincemeat. Early in November the two fat pigs had been killed and the big flitches of bacon hung on the kitchen wall. The kitchen table was pulled out into the middle of the room so that we never touched the flitches as we sat down to breakfast, or afterwards as we stood up again.

Breakfast was a serious and important meal, consisting always of rashers of bacon, and hens' or ducks' eggs fried in the lard fat that was generously swimming over thick slices of freshly-baked bread on our plates.

The bacon was cured with brine. It was turned and rubbed with the brine daily for a fortnight, then a couple of times within two or three days, and finally hung to dry on the kitchen wall to be cut and used as needed.

Dad always had one fat pig, and at most times two, ready for slaughter. The slaughtering was always done in the winter, or at least in a month with an 'r' in it, and there was no way that pig-curing in the summer would be risked.

As well as the flitches of bacon, there were the hams as well. Dad guarded the hams and no-one touched them – not even Dad, except on special occasions like Christmas. They were pickled in a mixture of brown sugar, vinegar, salt, saltpetre and bay salt, and during the process were rubbed and prodded to get the brine in and the blood and the impurities out. Then after five weeks they were strung up on the kitchen wall like the bacon flitches, with a strip of wood behind them to keep them off the wall and to allow air to circulate around them. My! If you brushed by in a hurry to meals, and the strip of wood dropped out, you were for it!

The village Christmas party was a great occasion for us children. On the Saturday after Christmas, Dad would turn the pony-trap upside-down, take the wheels off, grease the axle, and put the wheels back on. Both Billy the pony and the harness had a check too, all ready for the trip to the village.

At about 3.30 in the afternoon, we would drive off across the fields bound for Souldern. Billy put his best foot forward and we entered Souldern just as it was getting dusk. We stabled Billy in Bates Yard, then off we went to the school. All the village children were there, from three years to fourteen years old, and we joined our friends in the school yard showing one another our Christmas presents. In my case I usually had a knife, a tie or a book, and sometimes a diary.

Then into school we went, where the Christmas tree, about twenty feet high and decorated and lit with candles, was standing in one corner. A trestle table stretched the length of the big room. We all sat on forms and the bun fight started, with sandwiches, cakes, biscuits, jellies and cups of tea. We had to take our own plates, cups and spoons.

After about an hour of eating and chit-chat, we went outside until about 6.30, then back in again for presents and a sing-song with carols. An orange and a bag of peanuts was given to each child as we went home.

Billy would be hooked up to the trap again, and once out of the village he would be given a free rein. He could see his way home better than we could!

from

CANDLEFORD GREEN
FLORA THOMPSON

In earlier extracts from the Lark Rise to Candleford
*trilogy, Flora Thompson, through the childhood eyes of the
fictional Laura, describes some of the events which helped
to brighten the festive season at Lark Rise – in reality,
the Oxfordshire hamlet of Juniper Hill where she was
born. Now, as related in the third part of the trilogy, Laura
is a teenager working with Miss Lane, the postmistress
at Candleford Green, who not only runs the post office
but is the owner of the adjacent village forge. It is around
Christmastime, and the wintry weather is making its mark.*

One cold winter morning, when snow was on the
ground and the ponds were iced over, Laura, in mittens and a scarf, was sorting the early morning mail
and wishing that Zillah would hurry with the cup of
tea she usually brought her at that time.

The hanging oil lamp above her head had scarcely
had time to thaw the atmosphere, and the one uni-
formed postman at a side bench, sorting his letters
for delivery, stopped to thump his chest with his arms
and exclaim that he'd be jiggered, but it was a fact
that on such mornings as this there was bound to be
a letter for every house, even for those which did not

have one once in a blue moon. 'Does it on purpose, I s'pose,' he grumbled.

The two women letter-carriers, who had more reason than he to complain, for his round was mostly by road and theirs were cross-country, worked quietly at their bench. The elder, Mrs Gubbins, had got herself up to face the weather by tying a red knitted shawl over her head and wearing the bottoms of a man's corduroy trouser-legs as gaiters. Mrs Macey had brought an old, moth-eaten fur tippet which smelt strongly of camphor. As the daylight increased, the window became a steely grey square with wads of snow at the corners of the panes. From beyond it came the crunching sound of cart-wheels on frozen snow. Laura turned back her mittens and rubbed her chilblains.

Then, suddenly, the everyday dullness of work before breakfast was pierced by a low cry of distress from the younger postwoman. She had an open letter in her hand and evidently it contained bad news, but all she would say in answer to sympathetic inquiries was: 'I must go. I must go at once. Now, immediately.'

Go at once? Go where? And why? How could she go anywhere but on her round? Or leave her letters half sorted? These were the shocked questions the eyes of the other three asked each other. When Laura suggested calling Miss Lane, Mrs Macey exclaimed: 'No, don't call her here, please. I must see her alone and in private. And I shan't be able to take out the letters this morning. Oh, dear! Oh, dear! What's to be done?'

Miss Lane was downstairs and alone in the kitchen, with her feet on the fender, sipping a cup of tea. Laura had expected she would be annoyed at being disturbed before her official hours, but she did not even seem to be surprised, and in a few moments had Mrs Macey in a chair by the fire and was holding a cup of hot tea to her lips. 'Come. Drink this,' she said. 'Then tell me about it.' Then to Laura, who had already reached the door on the way back to her sorting: 'Tell Zillah not to begin cooking breakfast until I tell her to,' and as an afterthought: 'Say she is to go upstairs and begin getting my room ready for turning out,' a message which, when delivered, annoyed Zillah exceedingly, for she knew, and she knew Laura would guess, that the upstairs work was ordered to prevent listening at keyholes.

The sorting was finished, the postman had gone reluctantly out, five minutes late, and old Mrs Gubbins was pretending to hunt for a lost piece of string in order to delay her own exit, when Miss Lane came in and carefully shut the door after her.

'What? Not out yet, Mrs Gubbins?' she asked coldly, and Mrs Gubbins responded to the hint, banging the door behind her as the only possible expression of her frustrated curiosity.

'Here's a pretty kettle of fish! We're in a bit of a fix, Laura. Mrs Macey won't be able to do her round this morning. She's got to go off by train at once to see her husband, who's dangerously ill. She's gone home now to get Tommy up and get ready. She's taking him with her.'

'But I thought her husband was abroad,' said the puzzled Laura.

'So he may have been at one time, but he isn't now. He's down in Devonshire, and it'll take her all day to get there, and a cold, miserable journey it'll be for the poor soul. But I'll tell you more about that later. The thing now is, what we are going to do about the letters and Sir Timothy's private postbag. Zillah shan't go. I wouldn't demean myself to ask her, after the disgraceful way she's been banging about upstairs, not to mention her bad feet and her rheumatism. And Minnie's got a bad cold. She couldn't take out the telegrams yesterday, as you know, and nobody can be spared from the forge with this frost, and horses pouring in to be rough-shod; and every moment it's getting later, and you know what old Farmer Stebbing is: if his letters are ten minutes late, he writes off to the Postmaster General, though, to be sure, he might make some small allowance this morning for snow and late mails. What a fool I must have been to take on this office. It's nothing but worry, worry, worry.'

'And I suppose I couldn't be spared to go?' asked Laura tentatively. Miss Lane was inclined to reconsider things if she appeared too eager. But now, to her great delight, that lady said, quite gratefully, 'Oh, *would* you? And you don't think your mother would mind? Well, that's a weight off my mind! But you're not going without some breakfast inside you, time or no time, for all the farmers and squires in creation.' Then, opening the door, 'Zillah! Zillah! Laura's breakfast at

'Poor birds! With the earth frozen and the ponds iced over…'

once! And bring plenty. She's going out on an errand for me. Bacon and two eggs, and make haste, please.'

Laura ate her breakfast and dressed herself in her warmest clothes, with the addition of a sealskin cap and tippet Miss Lane insisted upon lending her, and hurried out into the snowy world, a hind let loose, if ever there was one.

As soon as she had left the village behind, she ran, kicking up the snow and sliding along the puddles, and managed to reach Farmer Stebbing's house only a little later than the time appointed for the delivery of his letters in the ordinary way by the post office authorities. Then across the park to Sir Timothy's mansion and on to his head gardener's house and the home farm and half a dozen cottages, and her letters were disposed of.

Laura never forgot that morning's walk. Fifty years later she could recall it in detail. Snow had fallen a few days earlier, then had frozen, and on the hard crust yet more snow had fallen and lay like soft feathery down, fleecing the surface of the level open spaces of the park and softening the outlines of hillocks and fences. Against it the dark branches and twigs of the trees stood out, lacelike. The sky was low and grey and soft-looking as a feather bed.

Her delivery finished, and a little tired from her breathless run, she stopped where her path wound through a thicket to eat the crust and apple she had brought in her pocket. It was an unfrequented way, and the only human footprints to be seen were her own, but she was not alone in that solitude. Everywhere, on the track and beneath the trees, the snow was patterned with tiny claw-marks, and gradually she became aware of the subdued, uneasy fluttering and chirping noises of birds sheltering in the undergrowth. Poor birds! With the earth frozen and the ponds iced over, it was indeed the winter of their discontent, but all she could do for them was to scatter a few crumbs on the snow.

The rabbits were better off: they had their deep warm burrows; and the pheasants knew where to go for the corn the gamekeeper spread for them in such weather. She could hear the *honk* of a pheasant somewhere away in the woods, and the cawing of rooks passing overhead, and Sir Timothy's stable clock chiming eleven. Time for her to be going!

CHRISTMAS GREETINGS
FROM A FAIRY TO A CHILD

LEWIS CARROLL

*Charles Lutwidge Dodgson, who of course wrote under
the pseudonym Lewis Carroll, indelibly implanted
his name on English literature when he wrote* Alice's
Adventures in Wonderland, *although he also produced
many other notable works of prose and poetry. He studied
at Christ Church, Oxford, and went on to become a lec-
turer in mathematics there, as well as holding several other
college appointments. He was ordained by the Bishop
of Oxford three days before Christmas in 1861, and his
seasonal poem reproduced here illustrates not only his
deep religious conviction, but his lifelong enjoyment of the
companionship of children, for whom so much of his literary output was intended.*

Lady dear, if Fairies may,
For a moment lay aside
Cunning tricks and elfish play,
'Tis a happy Christmastide.

We have heard the children say –
Gentle children, whom we love –
Long ago on Christmas Day,
Came a message from above.

Still, as Christmastide comes round,
They remember it again –
Echo still the joyful sound,
'Peace on earth, goodwill to men!'

Yet the hearts must childlike be
Where such heavenly guests abide:
Unto children, in their glee,
All the year is Christmastide!

Thus, forgetting tricks and play
For a moment, Lady dear,
We would wish you, if we may,
Merry Christmas, glad New Year!

AKNOWLEDGEMENTS

Introductory sections are by David Green, using published and unpublished reference material and personal interviews.

The extracts from *Lark Rise* and *Candleford Green* are from the trilogy *Lark Rise to Candleford* by Flora Thompson (1945) and are reprinted by permission of Oxford University Press. *The Christmas Book* by Gyles Brandreth was published in 1984 by Robert Hale, and the extract is reprinted by permission of the author. The assistance of Don Rouse of the Bampton Mummers is acknowledged for the account of the Mummers' Christmas activities. 'The Christmas Tree' is reproduced from *The Complete Poems of C. Day Lewis* (Sinclair-Stevenson, 1992). *The Englishman's Christmas* by J.A.R. Pimlott was published by The Harvester Press in 1978. The two extracts from it are reprinted with acknowledgement to the author and to his son, Dr Ben Pimlott. *Winter in Thrush Green* by Miss Read (© 'Miss Read', 1961) was published by Michael Joseph in 1961, and the extract is reproduced by permission of Penguin Books Ltd. The

Henley Standard is acknowledged for 'Henley's Victory Christmas' by Ian Fox. *Village Song and Culture* by Michael Pickering was published by Croom Helm in 1982 and the extracts are reprinted by permission of the publishers. The passage from *Pit Pat, the Pan's Hot* is reprinted with acknowledgement to the author, Isabel Colquhoun. The poem 'Goodwill to Men: Give Us Your Money' is the copyright of Pam Ayres. The item from *The Story of Swalcliffe* is reproduced with acknowledgement to the author, Dorothy Davison. The poem 'Once Upon a Time' by Henry Chappell, the account of Christmas in Banbury, and the items in 'A Weather Eye on Christmas' by Ian Fox are from *Oxford Journal Illustrated* and reprinted by courtesy of Oxford and County Newspapers. 'Ghoulies and Ghosties' by Mollie Harris was published in *Oxfordshire Roundabout* in 1966 and is reprinted by courtesy of the author. The extracts from *Lifting the Latch* by Sheila Stewart (1987) are reprinted by permission of Oxford University Press. *This Side of the Bridge* by Lilian Coulthard was published by New Horizon in 1982 and the extracts are reprinted by courtesy of the author. *The Father Christmas Letters* by J.R.R. Tolkien (edited by Baillie Tolkien) was published by George Allen & Unwin, and the extract reprinted by permission of Harper Collins. *Jog-Trot Days* by Wilfred Burson was published by Bodkin Bookshop and Gallery of Chipping Norton in 1980 and is quoted by permission of the author. 'Well, So That is That' is from *Collected Longer Poems* by W.H.

Auden, published by Faber & Faber. The extracts
from *Eliza of Otmoor* by Phyllis Surman, are reprinted
by courtesy of David Surman. The anonymous poem
'Preparations' is reproduced by courtesy of Christ
Church, Oxford (Music MSS 736–738). The passages
from *Linger Awhile* by Jack Callow are reproduced
by courtesy of the author. The poem 'Christmas
Greetings From a Fairy to a Child' by Lewis Carroll is
from a documentary collection relating to the writer
at Christ Church, Oxford.

Although considerable effort has been made
to trace and contact original authors, this has not
proved possible in every case. To those writers who
have remained elusive, the compiler and publishers offer grateful acknowledgement for the extracts
reproduced.

PICTURE CREDITS

Pages 15, 52, 181 – *Warwickshire & Worcestershire Life*.
Page 19 – Roy Barratt. Pages 24, 25, 26 – Novello
& Co. Ltd. Page 33 – By J.S. Goodall by permission
of Penguin Books Ltd. Pages 37, 58, 92, 93, 99, 112,
151 – Oxfordshire Photographic Archive. Page 48 –
The Lord Saye & Sele. Page 67 – Layston Productions
Ltd. Pages 75, 166 – Oxford & County Newspapers.
Page 105 – Colebrook & Co. Collection. Page 111 –
By courtesy of Wilfred Burson. Page 120 – English
Heritage. Page 121 – The National Trust. Page 124 –
Diocese of Oxford. Page 130 – Lilian B. Coulthard.
Page 138 – The Administrator of Blenheim Palace.
Page 147 – Harper Collins. Page 154, 155, 157, 159 –
Frank Packer / Oxfordshire Photographic Archive.
Page 171 – David Surman.

Visit our website and discover thousands of
other History Press books.

www.thehistorypress.co.uk

Printed in Great
Britain
by Amazon

31944260R00112